The Plan of Malden by Peter Tufts, Jr., made in accordance with a resolution of the General Court in 1794, is the earliest representation of the town known to exist. Only three copies are believed to have been preserved. The original is in the Massachusetts Archives and the Malden Public Library owns the remaining two, identified as the Richardson and Sargent copies.

Malden

*from primitive past
to progressive present*

Malden

*from primitive past
to progressive present*

by
Ruth Kimball Randall

In Recognition of
MALDEN'S
325th ANNIVERSARY
and
BICENTENNIAL CELEBRATION

published for the
MALDEN HISTORICAL SOCIETY
by
PHOENIX PUBLISHING
Canaan, New Hampshire

CONTENTS

In Gratitude	vii
Publishers' Foreword	ix
Introduction	xi
Part I Beginnings	1
Part II Growth	45
Part III The Troubled Years	97
Part IV Rebirth	117
Appendices	151
Mayors Who Have Served Malden	153
Commemorative Tablets	154
Bibliography	157
List of Illustrations	158
Index	161

Copyright 1975 by the Malden Historical Society

All rights reserved. No part of this publication may be reproduced, stored in a retrieval system or transmitted in any form or by any means without the prior written permission of the publisher, except for brief quotations in a review.

Printed in the United States of America
by Courier Printing Company
Binding by New Hampshire Bindery
Design and illustration by A. L. Morris

Library of Congress Catalog Number 74-30896
ISBN 0-914016-15-6

IN GRATITUDE

This volume has been, indeed, a work of devotion to the city of my birth. It still holds my interest since I continue to participate in the activities and serve in several of its organizations as well as hold active membership in Malden's First Church.

In addition to my Father's numerous scrapbooks (faithfully kept in order by my Mother during all the years of her husband's political career), his inaugural addresses and other public speeches, I am grateful for the assistance of many friends and acquaintances who so willingly provided information I needed to confirm necessary facts in several sections of this manuscript.

My thanks to Miss Dorothy L. Rothe, Assistant Librarian of Malden Public Library and a past president of The Malden Historical Society, for her genuine interest in suggesting the publication of this volume; to Robert W. Graham, President of the Society, for his encouragement; and to The Malden Historical Society and its special committee for willingness to publish this manuscript. My appreciation to Mrs. Walton S. Hall, first woman president of The Malden Historical Society, for her enthusiastic response and understanding. Her knowledge of Malden's background is legion, extensive beyond comparison. To my husband, Wyman S. Randall, my sincerest gratitude for his faith and encouragement in my undertaking.

My incentive for compiling this account of the city's development was two-fold. Initially, I had hoped to mark the 325th Anniversary of Malden's progressive growth, which culminated during the first half of 1974 in various observances by the first religious denominations: First Church in Malden, Congregational, and First Parish, Universalist, both one in the Congregational faith for nearly two centuries. The acknowledgement of this significant and notable event was the first incentive for this volume. The second goal became the real challenge to make the contents herein recorded sufficiently readable to arouse, hopefully, and stimulate the curiosity and interest of the younger generations, as well as the older ones within the community, that they might seek to learn, and in consequence, appreciate the background of the city in which they reside. If this latter prospect should come to pass, it would be my greatest reward for the infinite hours consumed in completing this self-imposed task.

Ruth Kimball Randall

PUBLISHERS' FOREWORD

One reason publishing town histories is so challenging is that they all differ. Unlike other literary art forms no rules dictate the range of subject matter, the narrative style, the form of presentation, or the overall concept of the book. Each town history must be a faithful record of that community's development, growth, and contributions to its society. Just as important, each history should be planned, written, and designed in such a way that it is responsive to the needs and interests of potential readers.

Unlike most New England towns which have published histories, Malden is a large city and has experienced many of the advantages and trials of urban areas. The diverse activities of her residents, the different nationalities which constitute the community, and the problems of growth all call for a history that bears little resemblance to the typical chronicle of the small New England village.

Malden's public and school libraries have long deplored the serious lack of definitive historical information about their city in book form. The author and the Malden Historical Society are to be commended for recognizing the need to research and write pertinent facts relating to Malden's more recent history before the records are lost. *Malden: From Primitive Past to Progressive Present*, therefore, represents a unique historical narrative which purposely avoids literary pretension but aims to present salient facts about the city's history in a logical, topical, format and sequence. In our opinion the purpose has been well achieved and this book should make a valuable addition to the library of all who have lived in Malden and want to learn more about the city's heritage.

Adrian A. Paradis
Editor, Phoenix Publishing

INTRODUCTION

It has been well said that "tradition is at the root of the community. It is tradition that gives a community and a church its history, its pride and its honor."

The Puritans who came to the new world were determined to form a commonwealth governed on Biblical principles and to enact their own laws. With a truly American religion set up and with Town Meeting instituted, the combination became a purely New England tradition. These Puritans were reformers and demanded strict adherence to their own polity and policy.

Thus, our forebears, who struggled to gather a church in order that they might create a town, were a group of determined pioneers and a people of strong convictions. In retrospect, with some imagination, it is reassuring to sense a degree of drama as we picture the beginnings of the struggling town of Malden on Mystic Side. It has had periods of great prosperity and about as many years of depression and lack of growth. The Rev. Henry H. French, D.D. once said, while pastor of First Church, "It is worth our remembrance that they had nothing for luxury and hardly enough for the bare necessities of existence."

A community develops with the changing aspects of each era, complete with its ideas, attitudes and patterns, each passing age a chapter in the overall story of many decades. Records of the growing town's affairs before 1770 disappeared years ago. Hence, church records, historical society reports, booklet articles, newspapers and family keepsakes have provided data for this version of Malden's historic background. We know that in the early decades, the price of growth involved strife and dissent at a time when each man in the small village had a share in deciding questions of the day. The minister, like all other men, needed to be a jack-of-all-trades to survive. Daily living in the mainstream of life was difficult, nevertheless, out of disheartening conflict, trial and error, neighbor judging neighbor, came a healthy and thriving community.

The bold adventurous spirit of great hearts, energetic leadership, and the profound spirit of tenacity, demonstrated by at least six generations of people, has written Malden's history. It has been written by great moments, rich deeds, lasting contributions generously bestowed, and the prospective revitalization of today for future prosperity. From the time of the first settler, imaginative minds of men and women, in a variety of occupations and professions, have created those motivations leading toward rewarding goals so necessary for the expansion of a flourishing community.

Firm foundations were laid to endure from the earliest times when Thomas Cotymore started the first mill in 1640, when Joseph Hills named the town, and the founders kept the faith to meet all adversities in a rugged struggle to overcome an "uncouth wilderness." There followed men like Job Lane, meeting house builder; Lemuel Cox, builder of Malden Bridge; and young pastors of the church who, in their turn, guided the spiritual life and civic life as they increasingly strengthened the growing village. There were the later inventive minds of business men like Jonathan Clark, the carpenter who constructed the first town hall; James Henry Putnam, pewter craftsman; Herbert Gleason, woodcarver; William Thomas Robinson, well-known artist; the Honorable Elisha S. Converse, Malden's first mayor and great philanthropic citizen; Deloraine P. Corey, the city's historian. There have been two citizens who became governors, the Honorable Alvin Tufts Fuller and the Honorable John P. Volpe. Each brought honor to Malden.

There are civic leaders, authors, educational instructors, city employees and the voters whose opinions express concern for the welfare of the city. We would not forget the women who have always organized, promoted and supported innumerable affairs and activities and causes within the city, harking back to their first petition of 1651. We remember the patriotic citizens who served in the armed forces in each succeeding war; staunch supporters and present executives in business and city government who are building Malden for today, tomorrow and for generations to come.

In its long history not a single monument has been erected within the city to honor any individual citizen for deeds accomplished. None has been needed, for every noble accomplishment has

Malden

been impressed upon the hearts of those people within the community who acclaimed them over the past three centuries.

In recognition of the 325th Anniversary in May of 1974, celebrating the founding of Malden on the Bell Rock hillside, which became the birthplace of civic and religious affairs, this account is submitted by a native daughter whose parents and maternal grandparents gave much of themselves in encouraging the best interests of the city and its welfare.

Malden's Puritan forefathers left an indelible impression that continued to flow from that hillside birthplace along the main currents with the development of the city for three and a quarter centuries.
"They builded better than they knew."

March 1, 1975
Melrose, Massachusetts

Ruth Kimball Randall

Introduction

Part 1
The BEGINNINGS

Gaining a foothold in America was a formidable undertaking, especially in the wilderness of New England where the winters were generally harsher, colder, and longer than those experienced in Europe. Colonizing called for bold men and women who had not only conviction to lead their lives as they chose, but also courage, resourcefulness, and stamina to achieve their goal. These brave Englishmen whom many of us claim proudly as forebears, left us a precious heritage, much of which still lives among many of us.

THE PURITANS, who paved the way for the settlement of the town of Malden, came to the new world "that they might worship God after their own fashion and order their lives as it pleased themselves."

When in the spring of 1629 a storm of persecution against the Puritans broke out in England, pleas were circulated urging Puritans to join the plantation in Massachusetts. A certain group of prominent Puritan leaders, men of wealth and culture, was strong in its belief that if the Charter were removed to America the colony would be free of English control and tyranny and the settlers in the new land could thereby form a Puritan Commonwealth governed on Biblical principles. Freedom of thought and worship would be assured in the new world.

Planting of the Colony

John Winthrop, having been elected governor of this new Puritan Colony, brought with him in March, 1630, the precious Charter aboard the good ship *Arbella* and touched shore at Salem, June 12. About 1,500 persons sailed with him in a fleet of seventeen ships. At that time there were well over 300 inhabitants living in the settlement of Salem, the majority of them either sickly or starving. John Endicott had arrived at Naumkeag, later named Salem, on September 6, 1628, accompanied by a small company of chosen men under a grant "to begin a plantation and plant the gospel." He was selected to govern the colony. Uniting with the few "Old Planters" already settled there, the colony numbering between fifty and sixty persons, settled under the title "The Governor and Company of the Massachusetts Bay in New England."

Discouraged by the unfavorable conditions at Salem, Governor Winthrop with his sixteen assistants, two ministers, and the other newcomers, left the afflicted little village and sailed south along the coast to explore the Charles and Mystic Rivers. In the month of July they arrived at Charlestown in twelve ships to join those already settled there. Even the uncouth wilderness looked hospitable to them after eighteen weeks in crossing the Atlantic. The struggling colony was soon troubled by lack of a good water supply. On invitation of Shawmut's only settler, the Rev. William Blaxton, the greater number of the new arrivals crossed over to Shawmut with Governor Winthrop.

By September 7 the new town, soon named Boston, was established. On October 19 the General Court held its first meeting. The

High Street from Market Square, Maldon, England, about 1900. The Moot or Town Hall with its projecting clock dial in the left center was built about 1440.

number of freemen in the colony increased to such an extent that the towns already settled agreed, as early as 1634, to send deputies to a general court. Thus a representative branch of the Legislature was established. In 1638, all the territory eight miles north of the Mystic River was granted to Charlestown and was known as Mystic Side.

In the first ten years of the Massachusetts Bay Colony 21,200 settlers, or about 4,000 families, had arrived. They came in 198 vessels and only one of them was lost at sea among this large number. Before 1649 nearly fifty towns had been settled in the Colony; twenty-seven churches had been gathered; trade with the West Indies was established, an exchange of furs for foreign manufactures and a flourishing ship building business commenced.

A military force consisting of twenty-six organized companies in four regiments, one in each county, together with a horse troop, was formed in 1643. It provided protection from the nearby Indians, the Dutch to the southwest, the French to the north and east. All this was begun before Malden was firmly settled.

With the coming of new settlers in succeeding months, welcomed by the few hardy souls who had remained at Charlestown, the colony grew and began again to prosper. When the earlier religious group, assembled "under the shade of a broad tree by the shore" crossed the river with Winthrop, a second gathering was organized, November 2, 1632. It was from this union, sixteen and a half years later, that a number of its members gathered into a church in "Mauldon." The desire to establish and maintain church privileges was the leading cause for the separation from the mother town of Charlestown.

In the summer of 1629 Ralph Sprague, with his brothers, Richard and William, four companions, and an Indian guide, was sent from Salem under orders from Governor Endicott to find good territory for new towns to be claimed for the Bay State Colony. Following an old Indian path, while bound for Charlestown, this scouting party became the first white men to travel through this country north of the Mystic River. It is believed that the Indian trail covered portions of Clifton Street, Rockland Avenue, Elm and Pleasant Streets. Passing through the region of what was to become the town of Malden, by a circuitous route, the party forded the river farther west in a later portion of Medford and continued along the westerly bank until they arrived at Mishawum. Sagamore John of Winnisimmet gave Ralph Sprague and his party "free consent" to settle at Mishawum where it is understood they founded the first colony there that same year of 1629.

Governor Winthrop led an exploration party through Mystic Side in 1630 and climbed Prospect Hill, now Waite's Mount, then west up through Middlesex Falls. He named the body of water he sighted, "Spots Pond." Impressed with the region he had surveyed, he petitioned the General Court to have Mystic Side set off to the inhabitants of Charlestown. The petition was granted in 1633, but it neglected to fix a definite northern boundary until 1638.

The story is told that when the authorities sent out a few men in 1635 to investigate the country north of the Mystic, the report was brought back that "having searched the first hills and finding a rocky and mountainous country, there would be little hope for the settling of a town beyond the mountains." (They viewed Waite's Mount and Boston Rock as well as portions of the Fells wilderness.)

There were many villages of Indians around the mouth of the Charles and Mystic Rivers. In the Blue Hills region the Massachusetts tribe claimed the area. The Pawtuckets lived and roamed through the region that became Lynn, Saugus, Chelsea and Malden, and even northward into New Hampshire. Legend says that the Indian tribe of the Tarantines from Maine provoked war on the Pawtuckets when they were already badly weakened from disease. They finally killed the chief, Nanepashemet, by a swift arrow through his heart. His

Bronze plaque depicting Governor John Winthrop's welcome to Shawmut (Boston) by Reverend William Blaxton is on Boston Common. Photo courtesy Wyman S. Randall.

widow, Squaw Sachem, ruler of the dwindling tribe, signed over most of her people's land to Charlestown authorities in exchange for twenty-one coats, nineteen fathom wampum, and three "bushells of corne." The deed is unique since it was the first and only document which conveyed the aboriginal title of our land to the white people. Very little Indian trouble was experienced by surrounding towns since severe plagues, believed to have been smallpox, had killed entire tribes during 1619 and again in 1631.

Mystic Side Early Arrivals

As early as 1631, only one year after the settlement of Charlestown, a few hardy settlers were living on Mystic Side in parts now known as Everett. That section of land lying along the eastern bank of the Mystic, later divided into Malden, Everett and Melrose, was originally a portion of the common lands belonging to the Charlestown settlement. It first appears under the name of "Mistickside" in 1634 when a section of this land, known as "the five acre lots" was divided among the inhabitants then living in Mishawum. Land on Mystic Side was apportioned among the Charlestown settlers according to the

Daniel Perkins' home on Appleton Street, a portion of which was built in 1647.

rules established by the Corporation before the Charter was brought over to New England. Four years later a second division, consisting of about 260 acres, was allotted to later arrivals. In the *Book of Possessions*, dated 1638, Ralph and Richard Sprague are listed as property owners in "Pond feilde," so named because of the several ponds found in the region. This additional acreage was awarded them in recognition of their founding of Charlestown. The later Melrose area was first known as Malden North End, then as North Malden.

    It is significant that most of the early settlements were made at sea level, mainly because communications could be more easily maintained by water. Roads were not built until some few years later. Disagreements were common between the General Court and the town. Malden men several times presented petitions for changes in direction of roads differing with those of the Court. Roads were not "laid out" until the 1700's. On March 7, 1712, the first appropriation of thirty pounds was voted by the town to mend the highways. What is now Main Street was laid out as a county road in 1806. Better roads were necessary when carts and wagons came into use. These were usually drawn by oxen, a pair as a rule, according to the distance or the burden with which they were laden. Citizens were required to furnish their own lanterns to light their way after dark.

Beginnings

It was not until 1640 that the "lots in Mauldon" began to be claimed. Thomas Cotymore, a Puritan sea captain, built a grist mill by the pond in Malden Square on a portion of the 35 acres of land he was awarded, and a dam near present Mountain Avenue on the easterly side of Three Mile (later Spot Pond) Brook, with a wooden trough carrying the water to the grist mill below. This early enterprise flourished for years, long after the death of its original owner. Scarcely four years after he had begun his mill Captain Cotymore was lost at sea off the coast of Spain. He commanded the *Trial*, the first ship built at Boston and completed in 1642.

By 1643 rude dwellings were scattered from the Mystic, near the Charlestown side, to Wayte's Mount and even beyond to the forests around Boston Rock. The early Puritans came by boat up the Malden River to Sandy Bank where land was reserved for a landing place and for a burying ground close by, or crossed by Penny Ferry and followed the wilderness trail on horseback through land now within Everett to the clearing around Bailey's Hill. A third route wound up the Mystic River to the point near Cradock's Bridge and followed along the Medford Road which led over a portion of what is now Clifton Street and on to the new settlement. Thus, by 1648, the seeds had been sown for an independent settlement and a struggling community.

These intrepid pioneers realized the possibilities of the land in the "uncouth wilderness" and found it to their liking. When the earliest settlers reached Mystic Side they found marshes stretching to the south down to the river and covered with an abundance of salt hay. To the north they saw open lands ready for tillage with a few clearings stretched along the traveled trails. There were wild grains and familiar herbs, many familiar and unfamiliar fruits, and game and fish "abundantly strewn about." Several ponds and streams were nearby and they found the greatest necessity of all, the clear water of good springs to satisfy their needs. Beyond all these "riches" for their comfort and protection (and eventually for their financial gain) stood dense woodlands.

Philip Drinker was the first to operate the Penny Ferry on the Mystic River (about where the Malden Bridge was later built) and this service continued until 1787. Peter Tufts succeeded Drinker in 1647 and became a large landholder on Mystic Side, acquiring an easterly portion of Medford land. When Malden Bridge was built in 1788, eliminating the Penny Ferry, tolls were required which became a burden to the townspeople. A round trip to Boston cost 47 cents. These tolls (Malden had two toll bridges) slowed growth for a time because money was scarce.

For well over a century Malden inhabitants had little worldly goods or ready cash. Most exchange was by barter. Late in 1640 (October 7th) the General Court issued a decree making corn, cattle, fish and other commodities legal tender for debts, and by 1712 paper money filled the same need.

Founding of Church and Town

During 1648 the dwellers on Mystic Side, then about 40 in number, asked to be allowed to withdraw from the congregation at Charlestown in as much as they had grown into a real settlement. The trip to Charlestown was long and tiresome, often dangerous, especially when families had children to carry. They wanted to worship in a way that would be convenient for their families. It was intended that a church should be organized on Mystic Side when there were sufficient inhabitants as required by the authorities. In 1638 the town of Charlestown had voted that the land on Mystic Side be reserved "for such desirable persons as should be received in it—such as may come with another minister."

It is believed that by this time the small settlement had already begun some form of religious services which were being conducted by William Sargeant, a haberdasher. He served as their church layman and ruling elder and at times young students from Harvard College assisted him.

With foundations completed for the gathering of a church, measures were soon taken toward founding the town. "A committee was chosen from the inhabitants residing on the south side of the Mystic to meet three chosen brethren on Mystic Side to agree upon the terms of a separation and the boundaries of a new town." The agreement, dated March 26, 1649, provided the necessary steps for "a church estate." The next step was to carry their petition to the General Court. With the approval of the Council, dated May 2, and the consent of the Deputies given, May 11, 1649 (O.S.)*, the freemen of Mystic Side were granted "a distinct town of themselves." Thereupon the church and town were organized and incorporated.

Thus the founders settled across the Mystic in the clearings

---

*"Old style" used to clarify dates until the calendar change to our present arrangement. O.S. is found in Malden's early history as well as on a number of gravestones in the Old Bell Rock Cemetery.

allotted to them. No authority other than their own appointed members was sought and they drew up their own simple document of church organization, believed to have been patterned after the Salem form. The one definite requirement, following the law enacted at the second meeting of the General Court on May 18, 1631, was that voting in town meeting was to be limited to church members. A man took his vote seriously and when his church membership was questioned it seemed a major threat to him. Because the town owned the church and all church property, all church matters were settled at town meetings. While none but church members could vote, all the townspeople were required to pay taxes for the support of the church and all were compelled to attend church services. They held that none but members of the church should be admitted as freemen, hold important office or have a voice in town meetings. A town without a church was almost impossible. "The gathering of the church was the beginning of civic and political life—in it lay the roots of all authority—out of it came the town and state." Here, the "little church of Malden, with hardly more than a score of members, stood alone in the midst of the wilderness, which stretched from the Mystic to Reading and Woburn and from the sea to the frontier settlement and church at Concord."

The document of 1648 bears the names of ten leading men of the town and they, with William Sargeant, first lay preacher, may be considered "the fathers of Malden." Ralph Sprague settled on Mystic Side very early. His brother Richard soon followed. The third brother, William, settled in Hingham.

About this same time Joseph Hills came. He was a lawyer from Maldon, England, and became the town's first deputy and speaker of the House of Deputies in 1647, although a woolen-draper by trade. "His legalistic mind compiled the first code of enacted laws printed in 1648," and although he labored to perfect them, he was not given credit in historical annals. An excerpt from the journal of the General Court states: "May, 1649 . . . Mr. Joseph Hills is graunted, as a gratuity, tenn pounds, to be paid to him out of the treasury, for his paines about the printed laws." Joseph Hills was also captain of the Malden Military Company. He it was who named the new town after his birthplace. With him came John Wayte, son-in-law of Joseph Hills, owner of a large tract of land in the vicinity of Mountain Avenue including the high rock later named for him. Barely twenty years of age when he arrived in Malden, he became one of its most prominent settlers. He was one of the first selectmen (1651); town representative from 1665 to 1684, and speaker of the House of Deputies; first town clerk (1649), a

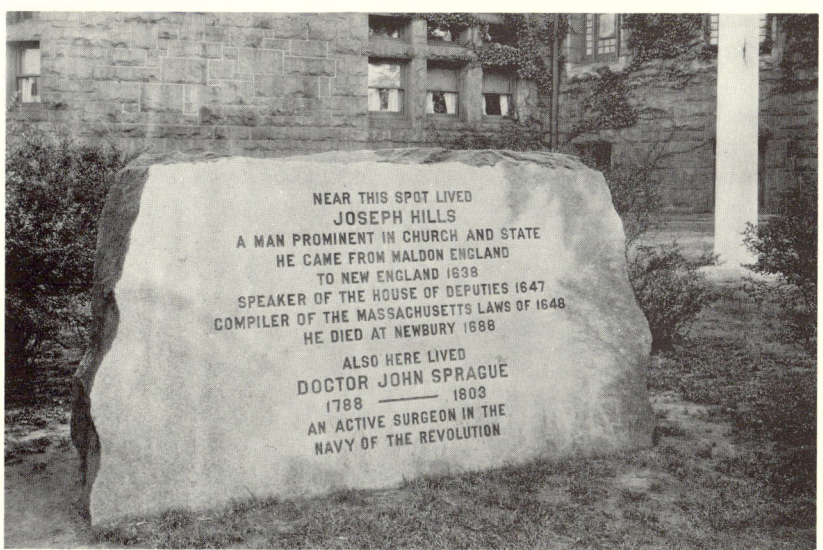

Hills' plaque, erected in 1924 on the south lawn of the First Baptist Church which was once Joseph Hills' farmland.

post he held nearly thirty-five years until blindness forced him to resign; and town representative to the General Court for eighteen years. This service became the longest term appearing in the town records. He was an officer in Malden's Military Band serving over twenty-five years.

Other early settlers included Edward Carrington, turner, who was active in town affairs and a man of considerable means; Thomas Squire, John Upham, James Greene, Abraham Hill, the earliest tavern keeper, Thomas Osborne, John Lewis, and Thomas Caule, Senior, who received authority to sell "bread and bears" in his house "to strangers." John Greenland, supposedly the first settler and a carpenter, built upon his land grant of 1638 near the south spring. Other petitions for the "lots of 1640" included: William Brackenbury, one in the party sent out on the 1635 expedition of discovery; Thomas Ruck, James Barrett, Thomas Moulton, George Felt, Thomas Skinner, victualler, Thomas Lynde, Richard Dexter and John Chadwick. Many Malden families can trace their lineage from these men and from many others who followed. All residents of the city can note with pride the many instances where the names of these men have been remembered in the life of the community.

These early inhabitants were farmers, craftsmen, woodsmen,

Beginnings

and builders. They were compelled to use every skill at their command in order to survive. They laid out their farms and built frame houses; they created their necessary household furnishings and farm implements; they built mills; developed the clay pits and made bricks. From the thick forests to the north they were able to furnish the towns of Boston and Charlestown with wood and timber. They built rough roads from what were at first merely winding paths and erected a succession of gates across them at the prescribed intervals to prevent cattle from straying. This was a common practice until wheeled vehicles came into use when the gates proved to be a great inconvenience and were permanently removed by 1740. The town pound solved the problem of straying animals after the road gates disappeared.

Taverns were permitted as early as 1651, a customary and necessary addition to every town. They occupied a prominent place in the community where town affairs were discussed by the townsmen who gathered there for relaxation. At that time a tavern was a place for gathering news; often a place for housing and entertaining guests; a rallying place for patriotic meetings; a welcome shelter in bitter weather, and a gathering place between Sunday church services. Malden had several taverns or "ordinaries," as they were frequently called. The earliest one was licensed by the General Court after a request was made by the selectmen in 1657. Known as Hill's Tavern, when Abraham Hill opened it in his own house, it was conveniently located where the four roads met about where the old City Hall was later built. It was also known as The Rising Eagle and at one time as Kettell's Tavern. On two occasions John Adams dined there in 1766 and again in 1771. Another "ordinary" was located on the site of the present First Baptist Church. This too was called Kettell's Tavern. Two others were built nearer Maplewood. The Half Moon opened in 1707 at Salem and Porter Streets and was operated by four generations of the Newhall family. In 1775 while run by Dr. Jonathan Porter, a town physician, wounded soldiers were treated there after the battle of Bunker Hill. Two others, Columbian and Pratt Taverns, were later occupied by business firms and used at times for social gatherings since they were near the center of the town. It was not too many years ago that the last of these public gathering places was demolished.

Near Hill's Tavern the stocks and whipping post were erected beneath a balm of Gilead tree. This form of punishment was continued until outlawed in 1777. The law was strict, swift, and unbending when crimes were committed. As early as 1653, a Malden resident was fined five shillings for "defect in stocks." In 1651 Richard Adams became the

Hill's Tavern, built about 1725 on the site of City Hall, was moved to Irving Street and later destroyed.

first constable of the town since with the erection of these implements a law enforcement officer was required. He was empowered with numerous duties as prescribed by the General Court. He administered all punishments handed down by the Court, using the stocks and whipping post when he felt it necessary. He was coroner, server of writs, collector of taxes, and executioner. By 1680 two constables were required since the town had grown and houses were widely scattered. Often men preferred to pay a fine (five pounds) rather than fill the unpopular office and sometimes a substitute was hired by a townsman who had been appointed, but was unwilling, to accept the duties.

Many early inhabitants on Mystic Side were non-Puritans. They had come to fish, gather furs, cut timber, and enjoy new freedom. Cod was plentiful along the shores and became the product which provided many men with a sufficient means of livelihood. Timber from the wooded area of what later became "the Fells" was cut and carted to Charlestown to sell. The streams were good flaxing places for the women. Bricks were made wherever the materials were available at the clay pits of the town. During 1795-1797 timber was drawn from the woodlands of North Malden by yoke of oxen and ferried to Charlestown to be used in the construction of the U. S. Frigate *Constitution*.

Beginnings

The Day of Doom:

OR, A
DESCRIPTION
Of the Great and Last
Judgment.
WITH
A SHORT DISCOURSE
ABOUT
ETERNITY.

Eccles. 12. 14.

For God shall bring every work into Judgment, with every secret thing, whether it be good, or whether it be evil.

LONDON,

Printed by *W.G.* for *John Sims*, at the *Kings-Head* at *Sweetings Alley-end* in *Cornhill,* next House to the *Royal-Exchange,* 1673.

Michael Wigglesworth, second minister at Malden (1655-1705) published his first "best seller" THE DAY OF DOOM in 1662. It required ten editions to satisfy the demand.

Early Military Units—King Philip's War

In 1675 King Philip's War broke out when "that crafty Chief of the Pokanoket tribe took to the war path for the purpose of exterminating the Colony." When the news reached Massachusetts Bay, orders were issued for a hundred men, and to this number another hundred volunteered. Malden men enlisted, some as "foote" soldiers and some as a cavalry troop. Under special orders from the General Court a petition had been presented by men from Malden, Reading, Rumney Marsh and "Linn," to form a Cavalry Unit in 1658 and thereafter was known as "The Three County Troop." It was composed mostly of those able to provide "some little elegance in its trappings." During its existence this unit performed well and was distinguished as "a band of stalwart Puritans who rode in the name of the Great and General Court as valiant troopers and as worthy Christians." Its cavalry flag was of crimson damask with silver fringe and bore a bare arm and hand issuing from a cloud and holding a sword. The arm and sword of that Three County Troop has been preserved as the crest of the state seal and on the coat of arms, adopted in 1780, of the Commonwealth of Massachusetts. The seal of the Massachusetts Bay Colony (1629-1684) was authorized in the charter granted to the colony by King Charles I. It was not until 1898 that the design of the great seal, drawn by Edmund H. Garrett, was made the official representation of the coat of arms of the state. Malden holds some degree of association with this state design since many of her soldiers were in the cavalry division which carried the flag now emblazoned on the state emblem.

A monument in West Kingston, Rhode Island, marks the site of the Battle of Big Swamp. More than a thousand Narragansett Indian men, women, and children were massacred here in December, 1676. It was believed by the white men that the Wampanoag warrior, King Philip, was being sheltered by the Narragansetts.

Malden soldiers were at the attack made on the Narragansett fort during December, 1675. Among those killed was Edmund Chamberlain; wounded were Lieutenant Phineas Upham and James Chadwick. Lieutenant Upham died a year later from his wounds. Several men from the town were in the expedition against the Indians at what was later named Turner's Falls in recognition of the slain commander of the expedition in 1676.

Beginnings

Anxieties of the New Colony

The entire colony was alarmed when news was received in June, 1684, that the high Court of England had decreed that "the Charter be declared forfeited, and their liberties seized into the King's hands." Subsequently, the hated Andros was appointed governor, the House of Representatives was abolished, censorship was established over the press, people were menaced with talk of the meeting houses being taken from them, public worship was not to be tolerated, titles to their lands were to be of no value, and taxes were imposed. Home rule became a thing of the past. The loss of political liberty was partially compensated by freedom from the domination of the clergy. During the first generation, until this time, the clergy had ruled, even to advising the General Court which kept in close sympathy with the Puritan divines and more often than not followed their advice. Though for a number of years the people continued to be taxed for the support of religion, no one was forced to attend church or was discriminated against for religious beliefs.

On December 19, 1687, Sir Edmund Andros arrived in Boston to become royal governor of all New England. With his arrival the General Court ceased to exist. Now citizens were aroused and refused to obey the King's orders. Rebellion became action. Such tyranny as laid down by the King was not long endured.

On April 4, 1689, Simon Bradstreet affixed his signature to a proclamation which was, in truth, a declaration of independence. On April 18 people poured into Boston and seized and imprisoned Governor Andros and fifty others. On the nineteenth Bradstreet led the militia to the Old State House where, amid the cheers of freemen, the former magistrates were declared reinstated on their own initiative. The citizens established "a Council for the safety of the people and conservation of the peace." Bradstreet, then eighty-seven years of age, was appointed their president. Thus a provincial government was established again. On May 6 Malden took action and sent an appeal to Boston when representatives from fifty-four towns met to consider the situation. Malden had voted that the officers of that government elected in May, 1686, together with town deputies, who were never legally dismissed, should resume the government according to the charter on the 9th of May, "and, in so doing, we do hereby promise & engage to aid & assist them to the utmost of our power, with our persons & estates." Before action was taken news arrived telling of the accession to the throne of William and Mary with authority granted for the continuance of the government under the old charter until a new one should be invoked. The new charter, when it arrived, was known as the Charter of William & Mary of 1692. Under this document the provincial government was upheld until the Revolutionary War. Simon Bradstreet served as head of the colony until he retired from office in his ninetieth year. His death on March 27, 1697, marked the last of the original magistrates of the first generation of Puritans.

Meanwhile, Increase Mather, statesman, patriot, and clergyman, upon his own initiative but with the knowledge of the Boston magistrates, sailed to England to confer with the King. He worked for four years attempting to secure a new charter favorable to the colonies, laboring with great diplomacy with King James II, and after his death with William and Mary. Authority was thereupon granted for favorable continuation of the colony's government under the old charter. Little is known of this diplomatic endeavor of the Boston clergyman.

Though the town feared the terror that was plaguing Salem between 1688 and 1692, little effect of witchcraft was felt in Malden. One woman, Elizabeth Fosdick of Malden, was arrested and jailed and another woman accused of "consorting with witches." Shortly before his death the Rev. Mr. Wigglesworth wrote to Increase Mather revealing the concern of his conscience by stating: "I fear . . . God hath a controversy with us about what was done in the time of the Witchcraft."

Hills' Well and Town Pump

Joseph Hills' well, close by his house near the corner of Salem and Main Streets, later known as The Town Pump, was one of the sources of the town's good water supply for 250 years. After one hundred years of private use it was acquired by the town. In 1843 a wooden pump and trough was installed and it became a popular watering place for man and beast. Thirty years later the wooden trough was removed and granite substituted with the date, 1875, carved on its surface. When it became a street hazard and thoughts of removing it began to be voiced, the protest signed by 929 inhabitants expressed their contrary opinion. To lessen the outcry and encourage the retention of the popular refreshing implement a granite pump, matching the trough, was presented to the city in 1887 by a public spirited citizen, Walter P. Sheldon.

When once again an attempt was made to remove the old town pump 206 women signed a protest against such action when they

Town pump at the corner of Main and Salem Streets was originally Joseph Hills' well. Presented to the city in 1886 by Walter P. Sheldon, it replaced a wooden pump on the same site.

declared the pump "a noted landmark of historic relations and a fountain of beneficent hospitality." The women's efforts were effective for a short time only, for in April, 1894, the City Council decreed that the old pump should be destroyed to make way for modern street development with plans already approved for the widening of Converse Square.

Meeting House Hill

There is no record describing the town's first Meeting House, but drawings show a small log building with only a few windows and a door. It was set on Bailey's Hill near where Bell Rock Park is now located. The building was standing as early as April, 1649, on the westerly side of the hill close to what is now Main Street, for "in the report of the committee appointed to survey a way from Winnisimmet to Reading," it was mentioned as "the meeting house on Mestick Side." There is evidence for believing that there were some inhabitants on Mystic Side earlier than 1648, as there was recorded in the archives of the Commonwealth a protest to the General Court from those living in the sparsely settled area, dated May 16, 1643, against a proposed highway from Winnisimmet to Reading.

Here the forty or so early settlers met for Lord's Day services and the freemen held their town meetings for transaction of public business. Inhabitants from Medford, Winnisimmet (Revere) and Rumney Marsh (later Chelsea) were considered part of the Malden settlement. Up to the time these neighboring towns were incorporated or built a meeting house they worshipped with the Mystic Side people, were buried in Sandy Bank Burying Ground, and married by the proper Malden officials. By 1702 it was required that "Charlestown neighbors on Mystic Side be given free liberty to come into the meeting house and hear the word of God, and be seated, men on one side, women on the other, by a committee on condition of paying 30 pounds."

It was the prevailing custom for meeting houses to be built on "rising ground" and so Malden's first building was standing on the high clearing not too far from the Sandy Bank landing place. Thus, Bailey's Hill, later Bell Rock, became Malden's religious and civic birthplace.

The town's name comes from the Saxon, Mael, meaning a cross, Dune, a hill. Its location, for the meeting house site, probably influenced the founders since such buildings were usually built on a hill for protection and used as a watch house as well as for meetings. Possibly this elevated spot with its interpretation of "a cross on a hill" may have impressed the early arrival, Joseph Hills, who named Malden. In the 17th century the men left the meeting house first after services concluded. They made sure no danger lurked about before the women and children left the dark interior and for some years the men bore arms to meetings. It was in 1640 that the General Court ordered that every man should carry "a competent number of peeces, fixed and compleat with powder and shot and swords every Lord's Day to the meeting house." This order held until after the Revolutionary War. The name "Mauldon" was used until 1769, when it was changed to Malden in the town records. The original name, misspelled for many years, was finally dropped.

Beginnings

Malden's First Minister

The new town was beset with troubles from the beginning. Unable to obtain a pastor the townspeople took matters into their own hands after nine prospects were considered and ordained their first pastor, the Rev. Marmaduke Matthews, by the same procedure as that adopted at Salem of "laying on of hands" or "lay ordination." Protests soon became evident because of Mr. Matthews' "peculiar religious views," but it seemed to be his way of expressing himself rather than the contents of his sermons. The Great and General Court summoned Mr. Matthews and tried him on problems of theology, principally, for his "unsafe and offensive expressions in teaching." The protest was reported to the Court by only two Malden men, but that was enough to cause a tremendous disturbance. Both pastor and church members became involved in this unprecedented case and it attracted the attention of the entire colony. After long weeks of discussion, arguments, and accusations, the minister was fined ten pounds solely because he had allowed himself to be ordained without sanction of churches or authorities. However, having no property other than books, Mr. Matthews was unable to pay the fine.

Three prominent church members, Joseph Hills, John Wayte, and Edward Carrington were ordered to collect, proportionately, from the other ten or eleven brethren who had consented to the ordination of their minister. This was difficult and it took over ten years to secure the required amount, principally because money was scarce and the townspeople felt the fine was unfair. Finally in October, 1652, the General Court, in response to many petitions, remitted Mr. Matthews' fine and deducted ten pounds of the fifty imposed upon the church members.

"This was an intense conflict which the church was called upon to wage and the people stood firm in their fight for the independence of the individual church and for their own self-government."

The women, too, entered into the controversy expressing their sentiments rather forcibly. To voice their opinions—as women—in that 17th century was an astounding and courageous act! However, when their minister was summoned before the General Court to explain his religious doctrine, they dared to express their sentiments. On October 28, 1651, there were thirty-six determined Puritan women who signed their names to a petition addressed to the General Court on behalf of their minister. Although their petition was to no avail the women had taken a stand and had done their best to plead their cause. This was the first demonstration of feminine independence in

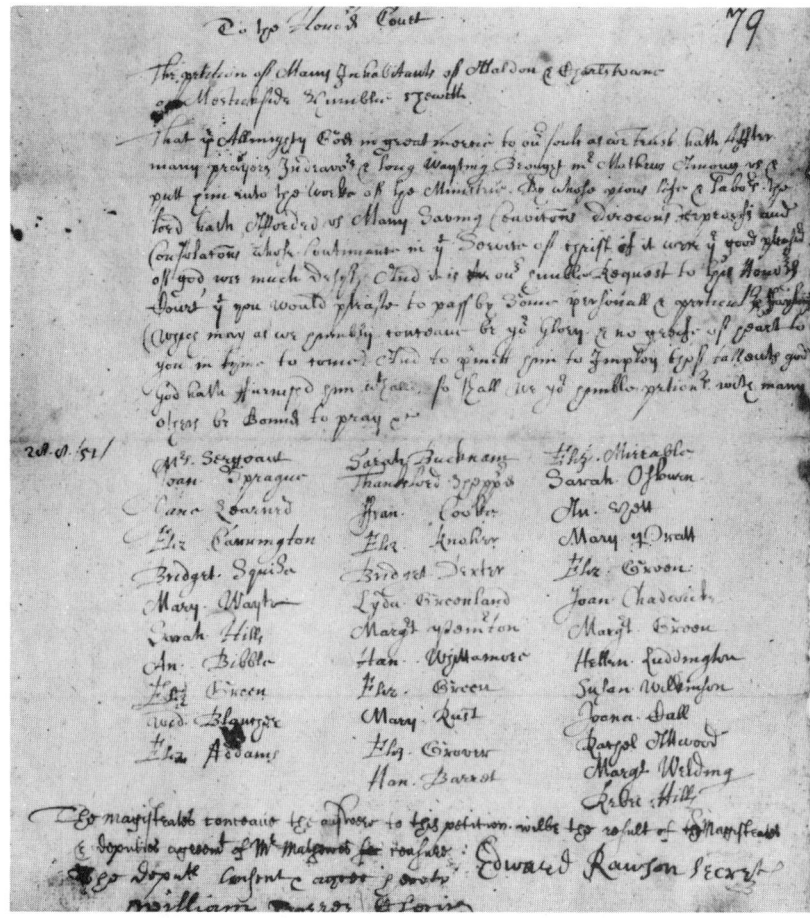

Petition addressed to the General Court in 1651 by 36 women of Malden pleading the cause of their minister, Reverend Marmaduke Matthews. This was the first known demonstration of feminine independence in America.

America and the first but by no means the last time Malden women would rise up to express their opinion in matters vital to the welfare of their community. A copy of the document has been preserved in the town's history and in the annals of First Church. A framed facsimile is on display in the Historical Room of the First Church, Congregational, on Pleasant Street.

Even in the midst of these church troubles, the selectmen voted in 1658 to build a new Meeting House a few rods south of the earlier one on the same Meeting House Hill. Though begun in September

Sketch of the second meeting house. Built by native son, Job Lane, in 1658, it served Malden's inhabitants for 71 years. Photo courtesy of Wyman S. Randall.

that year, it was not completed until late in 1660. This building was square and "tunnel type" like the Old Ship Church still standing in Hingham, the customary type structure built by most communities in that era. A Malden native, Job Lane, when only thirty-eight, was the builder of this "good strong Meeting house, 33 feet square at a cost of 150 pounds measured in corne, cord wood, provisions and fatt cattle." The complete contract, well defined, has been preserved so that the exact specifications give a true idea of the building which could accommodate about 125 persons. Nearly eighty families were living in the town at this time. Although "a territ" was specified in the contract, for some reason it was not built and the bell (one of only six in the colony at the time) was hung in a frame upon an elevated rock close by. Thus the location received the name by which it is still known—Bell Rock. It was not until more than thirty years later that it was voted at Town Meeting on March 21, 1693, that "ye bell shall be Hanged on the top of ye Meetinghouse." Several men, at their own expense and at various times, were permitted to erect horse-sheds "three foots and half in breadth for horse" by the Meeting House. Wheel carriages were extremely rare until the latter quarter of the century.

The second minister, the Rev. Michael Wigglesworth, for whom a street near where he lived and preached was later named, was no doubt the most famous man living in Malden at that time. Only twenty-two when he came to Malden, he was ordained as "teacher" in 1657. His pastoral duties were unfulfilled for seven years because of illness and three colleagues occupied the ministerial office during this period. When unable to preach, Mr. Wigglesworth spent much of his time writing. His most celebrated works were "Day of Doom" and "A Short Discourse on Eternity." He was renowned as a minister for fifty years; as a self-taught physician (principally because he needed remedies which proved successful for his ailment) and as a poet whose "Day of Doom" reached ten editions.*

The first of Mr. Wigglesworth's three colleagues, during his lengthy illness, was Benjamin Bunker, ordained "Pastour of the Church of Christ at Mauldon," on December 9, 1663, when he was twenty-eight. He died five years later while still pastor of the church. Mr. Bunker was the second son of George Bunker who came from England in 1634. He was one of the early proprietors who received land grants and he became one of Charlestown's and Malden's wealthiest and largest landowners. His holdings included the high ground named for him as Bunker's Hill in Charlestown. George Bunker died in Malden thirty years after arriving in the colony. Both he and his son, Benjamin, were buried in old Sandy Bank Burying Ground but their gravestones have long since disappeared.

The second colleague was Rev. Benjamin Blakeman who came to the church in 1674. He titled himself "Gentleman of Maldon" but he was never ordained while he "supplied the desk four years and left in the year 1678." Then in February, 1680, Rev. Thomas Cheever, son of Mr.

---

*The poem, Day of Doom, was Mr. Wigglesworth's masterpiece, the true embodiment of all that was terrible in the theology of the 17th century. The force of its awful realism (according to Corey in his *History of Malden*) made many a sinner quake with fear. This complete utterance of the belief and fears of Puritanical New England holds the secret of the great popularity of the less than rhythmic poem.

The Parsonage on Main Street near Bell Rock was rebuilt in 1724 and first occupied by Reverend Joseph Emerson. Adoniram Judson was born here in 1788.

Wigglesworth's old schoolmaster, began to preach. His pastorate did not prove to be too well accepted. Although he was ordained on July 27, 1681, after serving as stated supply for a year and a half, trouble developed because of "offensive words of a theological nature." He was given "a loving dismission" in the summer of 1686 and retired from preaching for nearly thirty years. Mr. Cheever went to Rumney Marsh, now Chelsea, and became the town's schoolmaster. He was most acceptable to the townspeople there and when the first church was gathered on October 19, 1710, he was ordained as its pastor. He remained there for the next thirty-four years, until he retired at the age of ninety. Two years later, on December 27, 1749, Mr. Cheever died and was buried in the Rumney Marsh Burying Ground which his son, Joshua, gave to the town of Chelsea in 1750.

The weekly sermon was the only intellectual life in the village for well over a century. The minister was expected to be "a learned man" to compensate for lack of education among his parishioners, and having contributed to the minister's "rate," these settlers felt they were entitled to a generous share of his knowledge.

Parishioners carried their noon day lunch with them on the Sabbath and had to be content with a cold one. No unnecessary work was permitted between sunset Saturday and Sunday night. All food

Reverend Adoniram Judson, son of Malden's eighth minister by the same name, sailed for Burma in 1812 to become the first foreign missionary. He translated the Bible into Burmese and compiled the first English-Burmese dictionary.

was prepared on Saturday and eaten in the Meeting House in winter or in the tavern where warmth was provided by the huge fireplace. In good weather people often walked to the Sandy Bank Burying Ground to eat the noonday lunch and to contemplate the many epitaphs and symbolic carvings on the surrounding gravestones. An afternoon service, nearly as lengthy as the morning one, required attendance.

The Ministry House

Opposite Bell Rock stood the parsonage where the early ministers lived. The Rev. Marmaduke Matthews was the first to occupy the "ministry house" after it was built in 1651. Following his marriage on December 27, 1721, the Rev. Mr. Joseph Emerson moved in with his bride, Mary Moody, daughter of the Rev. Samuel Moody, the famous and eccentric minister of York, Maine. This was but a few months after Mr. Emerson had been called to become Malden's seventh pastor. The present structure is the second parsonage (with but little of the original left) built after the earlier one was destroyed by fire on July 31, 1724, while the Emersons were occupying it. Mr. Emerson was held in such high esteem that the town immediately decided to build again on about the same site and the parsonage was ready for occupancy early in January the following year. This was the home of the ministers of Malden for 186 years. Later it became known as The Judson House since the Rev. Adoniram Judson, famous missionary and son of Malden's eighth minister by the same name, was born here, August 9, 1788. Privately owned after it was sold in 1837, it was purchased by the Baptists in 1948. It is now one of the few old landmarks in the city, a well preserved building that housed many ministers and their families in its parsonage days. During the Civil War this "ministry house" harbored fugitive slaves and served as one of the "stations" of the underground railroad.

Schooling Before 1800

Education stood next to religion in importance and, from the Puritans' standpoint, it became almost a part of their religion. Because it was believed that every good Christian should read the Bible daily, a law was passed by the General Court in 1647 requiring elementary schools in towns of fifty families and secondary schools in towns double that size. This marked the beginning of required schooling and laid the foundation for the development of the educational system in America. In 1663 Malden's opportunity for a free school was made possible when William Godden, "a roving trader," left the bulk of his estate in trust "for the schooling of the Poor children of Charlestowne and Maulden."

Malden was tardy in complying with the law. In fact on at least three occasions the town was called before the Court. In 1671 John Wayte represented the town fathers at Court for not having a schoolmaster, but apparently one was obtained after the town heard of the pending litigation. The case was dismissed after paying the court fee, however, in 1701 and again in 1710 the town was warned and fines were paid because it failed to obey the law.

Two requirements for applicants, no doubt, proved rather difficult. Before an applicant could be hired his hand-writing had to be acceptable to the Court, as well as a demonstration of his ability to teach the subjects of "reading, writing and ciphering." The selectmen were required to present the name of a chosen schoolmaster at the quarter session of the Court and the record states "his hand-writing was exhibited to the acceptance of the Court." In the case of another choice, "the Court liking his hand do approve of it."

"1691" seems to be the earliest entry in town records listing the fact that "Ezekiel Jenkins continuing to be the Towne's scoule master."

Headstone of Ezekiel Jenkins who died at the age of 57 on July 30, 1705. Photo courtesy of Wyman S. Randall.

According to this entry, it is assumed that he had been engaged possibly a year previously. He was paid three pounds with the additional stipulation that he have "ye benefit of ye schollars" to perform household tasks with Jenkins offering to keep the school in his own house in 1692, 1693, and again in 1704, serving until his death the next year. Men were hired on a yearly basis, although usually a session was from four to six months, rarely for an entire year's duration. School was kept in various sections of the town and records show that the town had a succession of schoolmasters.

    At least twenty were hired and served from Ezekiel Jenkins' time until Nathaniel Jenkins was hired in 1751. He held the post for the next forty years. At length, in 1711, the town voted "yt ye schoolhous shall be built 20 foots in length, 16 foots wide, 6 foots stud between joints," with thirty-five pounds to be paid for its erection. Because this small schoolhouse was centrally located and houses were widely scattered, it failed to serve the entire community. "Traveling schools" were begun with the hope of solving the problem. Both Ezekiel and Nathaniel Jenkins were given recognition for their schoolmaster days with carvings on their gravestones in Old Bell Rock Cemetery. The first school committee was appointed in 1789 and in 1799 the district school system was adopted.

A plaque on the Dowling Building, corner of Main and Pleasant Streets, marks the location of the first Malden schoolhouse.

Population Divisions

In 1695 another division, by lot, of more than two thousand acres of common lands among the seventy-four freeholders was granted according to the value of their estates, with an average of thirty acres to each man. The town voted that "John Sargent, Sen'r., is the man to draw the lots," a decidedly creditable testimony to his fairness and honesty. One, Thomas Newhall, was granted "a part of the common near his own land, providing he, his heirs and executors, set aside sufficient training place both for horse and foot."

In 1726, when that part of Mystic Side which had remained as a section of Charlestown was "set off to Malden," the town had a population of about 600 persons. This was the section now known as Wellington and Edgeworth, on the west side of the Malden River. "Malden now covered seven miles north, two miles wide, with 9,000 acres of land." This annexation seemed the answer to the many problems involving boundaries, church rates and location that had disturbed the town from the time of its earliest existence, but nothing was gained and bitter resentments continued. By 1727 portions of land to the north were set off, some to Reading, some to Melrose Highlands and Stoneham. Ten families, within an area of about one mile in width in the north end of town, were lost. A second portion was cut off from Malden in 1734 when the area known as Melrose Highlands was annexed to Stoneham. Another portion was added to Medford in 1817. Contrary to prevailing custom Malden and Mystic Side settlers did not build their houses close by the Meeting House or around a village green. According to the earliest plan drawn in 1795 by Peter Tufts, Jr., houses were scattered from the Mystic shores to "Pond feilde," later Melrose.

There were forty-eight Negroes living in Malden during the period of 1764-65. Several Malden families owned slaves, but by 1783 slavery was frowned upon and became extinct by state law. The last slave was Simon Knights who had been freed long before he died in July, 1847.

Church Division and "Conflict"

Bell Rock was Meeting House Hill until 1727. By that time the town had grown and developed nearer the center where the four highways, Charlestown Road, Salem Road, Medford Road, and the Reading Road met. The desire for change caused great discussion and many irate battles between the townspeople and the General Court took place for nearly two years. Because the town, after some 75 years, was growing in a more northerly direction, a new location nearer the center caused the division. When the altercation was finally settled, the original high ground noted as Malden's birthplace, was forsaken. This hilly area became a good spot for grazing cows after the Meeting House was demolished, and even after Malden became a city, Mr. Converse made use of this site for his herd of cows.

The dissatisfaction of a certain number of church members regarding the location of the third Meeting House created bitter feeling throughout the town. It caused the parishioners living close to South Malden (now Everett) to separate from the main parish. On September 13, 1730, they held their first meeting to organize a South Church. It took three years before a building was erected on "Sargeant's Hill" near Hancock Street and present Broadway. It was never fully completed nor was it kept in good repair, perhaps because it was a struggling parish for fifty-eight years. Beginning with sixteen male members and welcoming twenty-one others in 1787, the parishioners were not able to lift the burden or strengthen the church. They never held regular services for it proved difficult to find funds or means to pay adequately the two or three ministers who were willing to serve at various times. It was not until March 25, 1792, that the breach between the two parishes—South Church and First Church—was healed and they were once again incorporated into one body within the center parish.

The "bitter conflict" that divided the parish arose between those living in South Malden and families in the Center and North sections. Though the change of location meant only a distance of a quarter of a mile from the original site, it was soon apparent it would favor those on the northerly side of the town. The General Court was called upon to make the decision but time and time again it was changed, either by the Court or by the townspeople disregarding the Court's answer. Finally, the question was settled in favor of those living in North Malden. The Court ordered the Meeting House to be erected on the tract of land near the clay pits which had been conveyed to the town the year previous by William Sprague and his wife, Dorothy. It proved

A Word to those that are
afflicted very much.

A

SERMON

Preach'd at the

Lecture in *Malden,*

October 20th 1738.

On Occasion of the repeated and multiplied DEATHS of Children in many Families in said Town, by the *Throat Distemper.*

By *Joseph Emerson*, M. A.

Psalm cxvi. 10. ---- *I was greatly afflicted.*
Psalm cxix. 50. *This is my Comfort in my Affliction: For thy Word hath quickened me.*

BOSTON : Printed by *J. Draper*, for *H. Foster*, in Cornhill. 1738.

Joseph Emerson (Minister from 1721-1767) was the first to occupy the rebuilt Parsonage, and his son, William, was born there. William was the grandfather of Ralph Waldo Emerson and in later years became the minister at Concord.

to be a good choice after the structure was erected between what was then Lewis' Bridge and the Town Pound, about opposite the present Sacred Hearts Catholic Church on Main Street. This edifice housed the worshippers for nearly three-quarters of a century until it was torn down in 1802, when a new brick Meeting House was built upon the same site. This time all was harmonious as to the location, but change was in the wind.

During all the church "conflict" the Rev. Mr. Emerson, then pastor, was able to continue with his duties without any personal antagonism, even though he was greatly concerned and deeply distressed over the division of the congregation. Mr. Emerson was ordained Malden pastor in 1721 when he was only twenty-one. He served the church and parish for forty-five and a half years until his death. The father of thirteen children, several of whom became well known in later years, he was a fine scholar in his day, "a famous minister greatly honored by his people and by all the ministers in the New England Colony." The Emerson School was later named in his honor.

On Sunday night, October 29, 1727, all New England suffered a great earthquake. In Malden it brought fearful apprehension and many misgivings that God was visiting his wrath upon the townspeople because of their "bitter conflict" and church division. Days of Public Fasting and Prayer were seriously observed for several weeks, but all of the early fears of the event were soon forgotten and disagreements continued as before. In those formative years of "trial and error" small things like petty jealousies, irritating quarrels, and neighbor judging neighbor made life difficult. Town meetings managed not only the community government but regulated the social habits and conduct of each inhabitant as well. In the early decades the price of growth with its unaccountable problems, understandably involved strife and dissent at a time when each man in the small village had a share in deciding questions of the day. The minister like all other men of the town needed to be a jack-of-all-trades to keep the wolf away from the door. Daily living was rigorous and more or less restrictive.

In 1735 and again in 1736 a dreadful disease prevailed in Malden, affecting the children especially, with forty succumbing to the "throat distemper," later determined to be diphtheria. Mr. Emerson preached a sermon or two on the tragedy of this illness when several families lost three (one five) of their children to this malady in 1738.

Malden settlers were not blessed with much in worldly goods in those early decades. Mention is not made of chaises or chairs in

Malden until 1753 when three chaises and eighteen chairs (open chaises) are listed among those registered in the surrounding towns. Even at this time and for some years thereafter those who owned these vehicles were suspected of "a manifestation of inordinate pride or an indication of unusual wealth." The Rev. Mr. Emerson apparently desired one of these horse-drawn affairs for he recorded in his diary, "How much reason have I to watch, and pray, and strive against inordinate affection for the things of the world." His "affection" prevailed, however, for he purchased a "shay" in January, 1735. He penned his thoughts with these words, "The Lord grant it may be a comfort and blessing to my family." Nevertheless the perils of worldly pleasures soon beset the minister. Although none of his family were seriously hurt, the "beast" was frightened many times, overturning the shay and causing severe damage to the vehicle. At length, fearing bodily harm to those he loved and beset by mental anguish in indulging in such extravagance and causing the envy of his neighbors, he sold the chaise on June 4th to another minister who may have experienced the same quirks of conscience. Mr. Emerson's diary goes into considerable detail regarding his wheeled possession. "Have I not been too fond of this convenience? Should I not be more in my study and less fond of diversion?" Such were the perils of pleasure in the 1700's.

French and Indian Conflicts

During the French and Indian Wars, "Malden men were again called from their farms to perform military duty." In the various encounters which ended with the siege of Montreal in 1760, some seventy-nine Malden men were involved. The expedition against Cape Briton under the command of William Pepperell in the spring of 1745, when nine Malden men died during the "49 toilsome and weary days," was the cause of vexation among the people when Cape Briton was restored to the French in the fall of 1748. Many felt the agony and suffering had been for naught when the Acadians were driven from their homeland. Their plight was well recalled in Longfellow's poem "Evangeline" (1847). In the fall of 1755 vessels arrived in Boston with about a thousand of these exiles. Four families, numbering thirteen persons, were lodged in Malden for the next ten years, the town being required to house and feed them. The situation was not too well accepted because of the antagonistic attitude held against the whole affair. Malden sent petition after petition to the Provincial authorities requesting reimbursement for the cost of supporting the exiles living in the community. The requests were finally heeded and Malden received the reimbursements she had felt her due.

The names of at least twelve Malden men, of whom four were officers, appeared on the rolls of the army in the expedition against Crown Point and Ticonderoga in 1755. Some engaged the enemy on September 8, 1757, near the south end of Lake George, and another quota answered the call that same year when that French fortress was finally captured.

With more families arriving in the town and another generation assuming many official positions, moral and social attitudes began to take on a broader aspect. By 1767 Malden could account for: 191 voters, 127 dwellings, 7 work houses, 5 mills, 13 Negro servants, 84 horses, 100 oxen, 486 cows, 328 sheep and 9 swine. By 1776 the town population reached 1,030 persons.

Resistance Grows

It was more than a century after Malden had become a town before disagreements with British authority began to cause serious trouble. The penalties of taxes imposed by the Mother Country after King George the Third ascended the throne united the colonists and added a bursting spark to the smoldering fire which was rising toward colonial liberty.

One of the principal causes of the Revolution was the enactment of the Stamp Act in 1765. "No taxation without representation" became the popular rallying cry among the leaders in all the New England states and in Virginia as well, until the Act was repealed the following spring. "Liberty, Property, and No Stamps" were the key words in 1765 that united the colonists in their determination to reject all business activity that required stamps. Samuel Adams, called by some patriots a radical genius, by others a "rabble rouser," led the resistance. His call from Boston for action against British taxation created the desired results. Malden's representative was repeatedly sent to Boston to attend patriotic meetings in Faneuil Hall with instructions from Malden voters in support of the patriots' cause. Then new taxes were imposed on imports to America on such essentials as glass, lead, tea, paper, and paint. All the colonies refused to buy taxed articles and commodities. They stopped eating lamb so that their flocks would increase to yield enough to make family clothing. Homespun clothing became the fashion.

In January of 1770 a young new leader of eighteen, the Rev. Peter Thacher, came to Malden to preach. It was decided by acclamation that he was the man to fill the urgent need of the church and town. He was ordained in September and at once his influence became apparent. Under his able leadership Malden became one of the foremost leaders in the cause for freedom. Mr. Thacher was an outstanding patriot as well as pastor and his voice was heard in many of the surrounding towns, his opinion highly respected. He was gifted with remarkable eloquence and it was he who wrote the many expressive "Instructions." The forceful and moving words of the Malden minister became "the morning guns of the Revolution," described by some as "the preliminary 'Declaration of Independence.'" He was declared "the ablest preacher in America."

The growing problem of British taxes brought protests of immense magnitude. The tax on tea caused a terrific uprising. On the memorable day of March 5, 1770, the townspeople of Malden voted with a rising spirit of resistance, "that we will not use any foreign Tea, nor countenance ye use of it in our Families, (unless for Sickness) till ye Revenue Acts are repealed." Tea had been introduced into the colonies in 1720 and had become very popular. To forego using this favorite beverage was a real sacrifice. A homemade variety of boiled garden plants of various kinds was sometimes endured, but horrible as it was, it was tea of sorts. The staging of the devastating Boston Tea Party on December 16, 1773, threatened the safety of all the towns, Boston suffering the greatest aftermath with the closing of its port.

The Boston Massacre, although it sobered the populace for a time, increased the incentive for the colonists to arm and drill. When the hour came Malden townsmen were determined to resist the measures of British taxation. They got ready for eventualities with military preparations. Malden militia was ordered "to make a critical revie of the arms, ammunition and accountrements of every inhabitant; to enroll all men between 18 and 50; to exempt none from military duty under 60 years of age, unless exempted by law; to parade and drill the company twice a week." Two hundred and thirty-one men enrolled in the Malden militia and were ready to give their services, prepared for the struggle which they knew was bound to come. A "training list" numbering seventy-five Minute Men drilled under Captain Benjamin Blaney. Originally organized by Joseph Hills and John Wayte soon after Malden was incorporated, the Malden militia continued to be active as required by provincial law until legally disbanded well after the Revolutionary War, except for the brief period during the Royal Governors' terms in office.

Nearly every town erected a Liberty Pole, a symbolic image of the Liberty Tree of Boston. The meetings and patriots' agitation held under this famous Boston Tree created similar excitement among the surrounding towns. In the early days of "Auld Maulden" on the high hill beyond present Eastern Avenue and Hillside Avenue, to the south, stood a powder magazine and a Liberty Pole. The hill, called Powder House or Liberty Hill, retained this designation as late as 1890. The Liberty Pole was probably erected on the Malden hillside in 1774 or 1775 in conjunction with other towns, proclaiming the rights of the colonists to be a free and independent people.

With the growing tension the patriotic and fearless speeches of the Malden minister, the Rev. Mr. Thacher, fired the men of Malden with greater determination. Though they had felt somewhat removed from the spirited patriotic meetings held in Boston and more concerned about their farms and everyday sustenance, Mr. Thacher soon broke through the barrier and patriotism came alive in the town. During those stirring years Malden repeatedly backed the patriots' mass meetings. Their representative's attendance was the only means of communication in keeping abreast of developments.

As bounty for recruiting an army and purchasing supplies, the town of Malden raised what would have been equivalent to nearly $2,000 (of the then current silver standard), a sacrifice at a time when conditions were precarious in the entire colony.

During the early dawn of April 19, 1775, a horseman came riding furiously along the Medford Road crying, "the regulars are out!" He aroused those within Kettell's Tavern, the Meeting House bell was rung to alarm the town, and messengers were dispatched to summon the soldiers. The Minute Men, under Captain Blaney were mustered on the green in front of the tavern. It was late before the Malden company left and tradition says the women and children followed them for some distance as they marched to the beat of the drummer along the Medford Road and on to Watertown, then to Menotomy (later Arlington).

When well on their way toward Menotomy the Malden company intercepted twelve British soldiers who were conveying two supply wagons loaded with ammunition and provisions but had become separated from Lord Percy's forces. The Malden Minute Men took the soldiers prisoners and captured the wagons of supplies. Malden men were cited when this incident, which took place near the junction of the Lexington and Medford roads, was later recorded as one of the first skirmishes of the American Revolution. Malden Minute Men with those of other towns followed the retreating British troops after the

Concord Bridge skirmish, and created great harassment, causing the fleeing soldiers to become badly disorganized while on their harried march back to Charlestown Neck.

With British troops arriving back in Charlestown, women and children fled from there and from Boston, across the marshes to Medford and Malden. They were housed and provided for in the Malden Meeting House until danger had passed. This was a real act of compassion since Malden was as desperate for food as were many of the other towns at the time.

On June 17, 1775, Captain Blaney's Company was stationed at Beacham's Point on the Mystic River, near the Penny Ferry landing place. Here the men accompanied by their minister, the Rev. Mr. Thacher, watched the Battle of Bunker Hill. On the demand of the Committee of Safety, three ministers were requested to prepare a true statement of the Bunker Hill Battle to be sent to England "for the information of Posterity." Mr. Thacher's eye-witness account was judged so accurate that a copy was sent to England where it has been preserved ever since. It was considered the most valuable description of the events of that tragic day and in consequence, Mr. Thacher was granted "beating orders" by the Provincial Congress, a certificate permitting recruiting powers for the seacoast defense of Massachusetts. Captain Blaney's Company guarded the designated strategic point until the British sailed out of Boston Harbor. Mr. Thacher's Battle of Bunker Hill account is printed in Frothingham's *History of the Siege of Boston* 382, and in the *Historical Magazine*, 4 (Series 2) 381. The Library of the American Antiquarian Society has an original manuscript of Mr. Thacher's account.

Many residents witnessed the Battle of Bunker Hill from Wayte's Mount. This was a far safer viewpoint since the British batteries kept up a continual fire upon the few houses along the Mystic. People fled that besieged area, several were killed, many were made homeless.

Detachments of men and supply wagons were constantly passing between the eastern American lines and Cambridge headquarters. Powder Hill in Chelsea (where the Soldiers Home stands) was an excellent lookout. The hill was so named because early settlers bought it from the Indians for a horn of gun powder. Here on this vantage point, General Washington and his officers came several times to observe the action in the harbor. On the way he frequently stopped for rest and hospitality at the home of Captain John Dexter whose farm stood far back from the Medford Road (at Elm Street), its driveway

The 1848 Dexter home on Elm Street from an 1869 photograph. General Washington was often entertained by Captain John Dexter in the original home on this site during the Revolution.

lined with handsome elms. The Dexter home was a notable landmark, as was one of the elm trees well into the present century.

In spite of the general anxiety which prevailed during the day (Dorchester Heights being readied by American forces to surprise British forces and their general and which resulted in the evacuation of Boston), the Rev. Mr. Thacher was invited to deliver the annual Boston Massacre Oration on March 5, 1776. Since the British Governor would not permit this observance to be held in Boston's Old South Meeting House as had been the custom, Mr. Thacher delivered his oration in the Meeting House at Watertown. His fiery and inspiring address was considered of such substantial importance it was printed for the populace.

Commissioned by General Washington, September 11, 1775, Colonel Benedict Arnold assembled his troops in Cambridge for his expedition to Quebec. The first detachment marched from Cambridge on the evening of September 13, passing along the Medford Road to Malden where they encamped that night. The next morning another detachment marched through Malden. They were on the way to Newburyport where the 1,100 men boarded eleven vessels and sailed along the coast before tramping the Maine wilderness to Canada. Malden was a busy place while General Washington was stationed at Cambridge.

Beginnings

In 1776 there were great suffering and discouragement for the Malden people as they endured the reverses of war. The names of those who served are listed on a plaque standing at the entrance to old Bell Rock Burying Ground. The gravestones of some of these patriots are still visible within the walls of Malden's ancient cemetery.

Calls for volunteers were continually received. Malden, like all other towns, was required to furnish funds and supplies on several occasions. A contingent of twenty-four men marched to Ticonderoga in the fall of 1776. The Rev. Mr. Thacher gave the soldiers encouragement with his letters and news of their families. Thirty men enrolled in 1777 for a three-year period of service.

Several Malden men served in the naval forces and were in command of vessels, some were captured and imprisoned by the British but later released to return to Malden to live full and active lives in the town. Captain Daniel Waters and Captain Jonathan Oakes became two of Malden's most famous naval heroes. Dr. Ezra Green served as surgeon with Captain John Paul Jones, Dr. John Sprague also served at sea as did Isaac Smith, who, on retirement became Malden's wealthiest citizen.

Independence Is Born

Independence repeatedly became the subject of discussion at town meetings as the patriots of Boston stirred the populace to more and more action. With an urgent letter of request from Boston under the correspondence instruction of patriot Samuel Adams, urging instructions to their representative, "the men of Malden, impelled by the enthusiastic pastor, the Rev. Mr. Thacher, responded almost at once to a public call before all other towns." In the renowned Instructions of May 27, 1776, when Mr. Thacher and the men of Malden declared, "that if they [the Congress] should declare America to be a free & independent Republic your Constituance will support and defend the measure to the last drop of their blood and the last farthing of their treasure," Malden became the first town to issue their instructions, preceding Boston by three days. The eloquence and directness of orders laid down in these Instructions attracted the attention of Chief Justice John Marshall. He was so impressed with Mr. Thacher's proclamation that he used a section of it in his *Life of George Washington* (1804). The discourse, acknowledged to be of such importance, was lithographed in 1831 by means of public subscription. Copies soon appeared upon the walls of many a Malden home. A framed copy was hung in the Malden Public Library for the general public to read. The discourse was entered upon Malden town records and printed in full in the *Boston Gazette*.

With the adoption of the Declaration of Independence, a copy was sent to every minister in the Province to be read at the close of the afternoon service the first Sunday after it was received. "It became an historic occasion when an eagerly listening audience in the Malden Meeting House heard the heart-stirring document for the first time." This must have been a glorious moment for the Rev. Mr. Thacher and the other patriots of Malden.

In the fall of 1778 a guard was posted on Wayte's Mount to keep his eyes on the far distant high hill in Boston and to be ready to light the beacon erected there on Malden's high sentry post. This beacon was similar to the one raised some years previously "sett on Sentry Hill" (Trimount, Boston) for the purpose of warning the town and surrounding communities in case of enemy attack along the coast by British ships. The Malden Beacon was to be set afire when the signal was sighted from Boston's flame. Although warnings were signaled several times the Beacons were never lighted.

On September first of 1779, when the Convention assembled in the Cambridge Meeting House to draft the Constitution of the Commonwealth of Massachusetts, principally constructed through the wisdom of John Adams, the Rev. Mr. Peter Thacher was chosen very "properly" to be Malden's delegate. He had been so designated at the Town Meeting held August 12 in Hill's Tavern west room. Mr. Thacher took an active part in the discussions and contributed to the plans which produced the final document. When properly framed by the Convention, the instrument was presented to the towns and Malden approved it on April 30, 1780.

The people of Malden, like those in other colonial towns, suffered through many difficult years of adversity during the long struggle for independence. The war ended with the British surrender at Yorktown, October 19, 1781. The United States of America was formally recognized as an independent nation with the signing of the Paris Peace Treaty on September 3, 1783. On September 17, 1787, delegates signed the Constitution of the United States and when George Washington was inaugurated as first president of the newly formed United States, on April 30, 1789, a new era in American history had begun.

Life changed in many respects following the close of the Revolutionary War. A new era dawned, a new nation was born. The church and the town, through sufferance of hardships and the firm

Instructions of the town of Malden to their Representative, Passed May 27th, 1776:

Sir—A resolution of the late Honorable House of Representatives, calling upon the several towns in this Colony to express their minds, with respect to the important question of AMERICAN INDEPENDENCE, is the occasion of our now instructing you.

The time was, Sir, when we loved the King and the People of Great Britain, with an affection truly filial; we felt ourselves interested in their glory, we shared in their joys and sorrows, we cheerfully poured the fruit of all our labors into the lap of our Mother Country, and without reluctance, expended our blood and our treasure in her cause. These were our sentiments towards Great Britain; while she continued to act the part of a parent State, we felt ourselves happy in our connection with her, nor wished it to be dissolved. But our sentiments are altered. It is now the ardent wish of ourselves, that America may become FREE AND INDEPENDENT STATES. A sense of unprovoked injuries will arouse the resentment of the most peaceful; such injuries these Colonies have received from Britain. Unjustifiable claims have been made by the king and his minions, to tax us without our consent. These colonies have been prosecuted in a manner cruel and unjust to the highest degree, the frantic policy of Administration hath induced them to send Fleets and Armies to America, that by depriving us of our trade, and cutting the throats of our brethren, they might awe us into submission, and erect a system of despotism which should so far enlarge the influence of the Crown, as to enable it to rivet their shackles upon the people of Great Britain. This was brought to a crisis upon the ever memorable nineteenth of April; we remember the fatal day; the expiring groans of our murdered countrymen yet vibrate on our ears!! We now behold the flames of their peaceful dwellings ascending to heaven; we hear their blood crying to us from the ground, VENGEANCE! and charging us, as we value the peace of their manes, to have no further connection with a King, who can unfeelingly hear of the slaughter of his subjects and composedly sleep with their blood upon his soul. The manner in which the War has been prosecuted has confirmed us in these sentiments; Piracy and Murder, robbery and breach of faith, have been conspicuous in the conduct of the

King's Troops; defenceless Towns have been attacked and destroyed,—the ruins of Charlestown, which are daily in our view, daily remind us of this. The cries of the Widow and the Orphan demand our attention; they demand that the hand of pity should wipe the tears from their eyes; and that the sword of their Country should avenge their own and our rights, and to bring to condign punishment the elevated villains who have trampled upon the sacred rights of men, and affronted the majesty of the people. We hoped in vain. They have lost their love to Freedom, they have lost their spirit of just resentment. We therefore renounce with disdain our connection with the kingdom of Slaves; we bid a final adieu to Britain. Could an accommodation be now effected, we have reason to think that it would be fatal to the liberties of America,—we should soon catch the contagion of venality and dissipation, which has subjected Britain to lawless domination: Were we placed in the situation we were in, in the year 1773; were the powers of appointing to office, and commanding the Militia, in the hands of Governors, our arts, trade, and manufactures would be cramped; nay, more than this, the life of every man who has been active in the cause of his Country would be endangered. For these reasons, as well as many others which might be produced, we are confirmed in the opinion, that the present age will be deficient in their duty to God, their posterity, and themselves, if they do not establish an AMERICAN REPUBLIC. This is the only form of government which we wish to see established; for we can never willingly be subject to any other King, than He, who being possessed of infinite wisdom, goodness and rectitude, is alone fit to possess unlimited power.

We have freely spoken our sentiments upon this important subject; but we mean not to dictate. We have unbounded confidence in the wisdom and uprightness of the Continental Congress; with pleasure we recollect that this affair is under their direction:—and we now instruct you, Sir, to give them the strongest assurance, that if they should declare America to be a Free and Independent Republic, your constituents will support and defend the measure to the "Last Drop Of Their Blood And The Last Farthing Of Their Treasure."

determination of their people, had endured to meet the constantly changing conditions. The first century and a half was dedicated to religious and moral ideals, following the fundamental Puritan belief. The influence of the Founders left an indelible imprint upon succeeding generations, through all their hardships, they "builded better than they knew."

In 1784 when Mr. Thacher requested his dismission after fourteen years as Malden's eminent pastor, the citizens reluctantly granted his request. He became the minister of the Brattle Street Church in Boston. Though the people in Malden tried to persuade Mr. Thacher to stay with them, they soon reasoned that he would be given "a larger service in a wider field" and granted him a letter of "affectionate commendation" on December 8th. Because of the reluctance of his parishioners to dismiss Mr. Thacher the Brattle Street Church made a contribution of $1,000 to "console" his Malden parish. For fourteen of the years that he was pastor of the Boston Church he was also chaplain of the Massachusetts Senate, holding the office until his death. As chaplain it was indeed fitting that he should offer the prayer at the laying of the cornerstone of the Bulfinch State House on Beacon Hill on July 4, 1795. In January of 1791, Mr. Thacher became one of ten men to form the Massachusetts Historical Society, the first such society in the United States. He died in Savannah, Georgia, where he had gone for his health on December 16, 1802, when in the very prime of life. His name will forever hold an honored place in the annals of First Church in Malden and in Malden's history. Four of his children lie in Bell Rock Cemetery.

Lemuel Cox, Bridge Builder

Malden Bridge, which spanned the Mystic River at the place formerly known as Penny Ferry, was built in 1788 and completed within six months by Lemuel Cox, a Malden townsman. He was the contractor for this bridge and also for the Charles River Bridge. Lemuel Cox's great bridge across the Charles River between Boston and Charlestown was hailed as a real achievement. Built shortly after the Revolutionary War, it was regarded as "the longest bridge in the world" and considered "a triumph of engineering."

Mr. Cox was a celebrated architect and bridge builder. He gained such prominence that he was sent to Ireland where he constructed

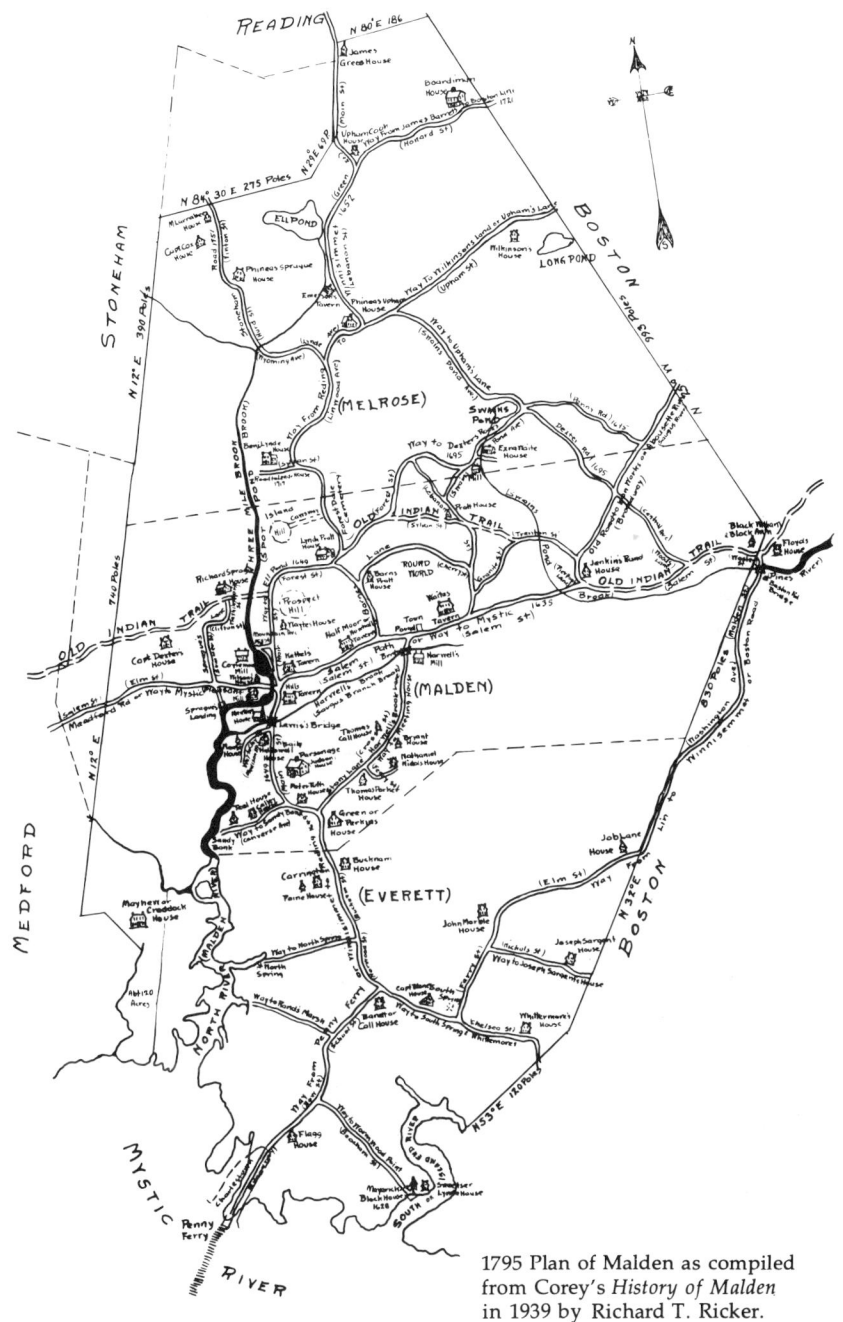

1795 Plan of Malden as compiled from Corey's *History of Malden* in 1939 by Richard T. Ricker.

Beginnings

nine important bridges. "The proprietors of Malden and Charles River Bridges voted him handsome gratuities in addition to his stipulated pay." Malden Bridge was 2,400 feet long, 32 feet wide, with a draw at the channel at high tide of 23 feet.

Part 2
GROWTH

During the nineteenth century the United States became the world's leading industrialized nation and more than doubled in size as pioneers gradually pushed her frontiers west to the Pacific Ocean. Unimpressed by promises of wealth or greater opportunity elsewhere, the citizens of Malden preferred to remain by their hearthsides to enjoy and perpetuate their New England heritage as they worked to lay the foundations for their city's growth and future well being.

DURING THE LATTER YEARS of the century the Congregational denomination, which had prevailed from the inception of religion in the town and continued for 154 years, began to feel the effect of other denominations. By 1785 the Unitarians had appeared. The present building, erected as late as 1878, corner of Hillside and Eastern Avenues, was the site of the first Unitarian Meeting House.

By 1803 changes in religious doctrines were being seriously discussed and several new denominations appeared in Boston. Congregationalism now became but one of many religions. This expansion of new denominations spread to Malden and the next few years found various religious groups separating from the center First Church. When other forms of recreation were permitted and became common with the younger generations, congregations grew restless and often rebellious under the compulsion of lengthy sermons and prayers. Gradually, services grew shorter and more "reasonable" in length.

The legal separation between church and state occurred in Massachusetts in 1833, and "by 1883 the last vestiges of aristocratic Puritanism were swept away." In 1803 the First Baptist Church was founded; in 1821 the First Methodist was organized. The Universalist Church and First Church, Congregational, separated in 1828. Beginning in 1848 and continuing until 1893, five other Congregational churches were organized, most of them from the membership of the First Church, namely: Melrose (1848); Winthrop in South Malden, now Everett (1848); Maplewood (1873); Linden (1876); Mystic Side (1893). With a population of 16,470 in 1886, Malden had eleven Protestant churches and one Catholic church.

"In the early days of the Irish immigration to America, some of these arrivals settled in Malden and surrounding towns." In the beginning, they were required to make the same tedious journey to Charlestown as had been imposed upon the earliest Protestant settlers before they were gathered into "a church estate." The spiritual needs of the "people of the Catholic faith were taken care of on one Sunday a month by a visiting priest. For the remaining Sundays of each month, these hardy Irish settlers had to journey to St. Mary's Church in Charlestown. Because the fare on the coach was too steep for most of them—40 cents round trip—the men and young folks walked and only the older women rode."

In 1853 these later newcomers were organized into a parish which extended from Charlestown on the south to Lowell and Law-

Central Square looking north in 1869, showing Waites block, the First Baptist Church and the Town Hall. Photo courtesy of the Malden Evening News.

rence on the north. By early 1854 Father John Ryan, the pastor, had collected sufficient funds to purchase property for the erection of a parish church in Malden. On Christmas morning, 1855, Mass was celebrated for the first time in the basement of the new church then under construction on Pleasant Street near the Medford line, later known as The Church of the Immaculate Conception. Masses had been held the previous year in Green's Hall, then standing on Pleasant Street about where the Dowling building was later erected in Malden Square. The three priests associated with the newly formed parish also conducted services each Sunday in All Souls Chapel standing on the grounds of Holy Cross Cemetery, Broadway, in Malden.

St. Paul's Episcopal Church had started in 1861 then became Grace Church, but in 1867 a permanent organization was established; St. Luke's Episcopal Church in Linden was consecrated in 1884 and the Young Men's Christian Association was founded in 1886.

The War of 1812

A conflict between Great Britain and the United States resulted when England attempted to prevent this country from trading with

The old Malden Bridge toll house, used until 1858.

France. The war lasted two years during which time the U.S. frigate *Constitution*, Queen of the Navy and nicknamed *Old Ironsides*, made history. Built in Boston and launched in 1798, some of the timber for the *Constitution* was drawn from North Malden from 1795 to 1797, and thus Malden made a valuable contribution to the frigate's construction.

Industries Developed

With the turn of the century the town of Malden began to lose some of its rural aspects as the people turned their attention to manufacturing. Below where Spot Pond Brook crossed Mountain Avenue, William Barrett established his silk-dyeing business in 1804 and it prospered until 1882. This dye house was standing as late as 1949 when it was razed and a parking lot has occupied the premises since the 1950's. Above the valley beyond the dye works stood a rolling and splitting nail mill, which became the first of its kind to cut and head nails in one operation. It was constructed in 1804 by the three Odiorne Brothers and their business was successful until 1838. Last making was introduced by Samuel Cox in 1812 and continued for some years.

Elisha S. Converse, from a photograph taken in the late eighteen hundreds.

Women took parts from small shoe shops located along Salem Street to sew on the backs or soles as "piece work" and to make money for their church missionary work. They received very small pay but "every little helped" to encourage them in their earnest endeavors. The manufacture of tinware was another industry.

Two factors brought greater prosperity to Malden: the opening of the Boston and Maine Railroad in 1845 and the establishment by Elisha S. Converse of the Boston Rubber Shoe Company in 1853. Under Converse's management this became one of the largest plants of its kind in the United States. Mr. Converse was responsible for its growth and development from 1853 to 1893 while he served as treasurer, general manager, and finally president. Among the early pioneers of the rubber industry, the company expanded in 1882 with the erection of a second factory in Melrose nearly as large as the Malden plant. It was rebuilt in a more modern style after a fire in 1875. From the sixteen acres representing the combined floor space of the huge factories in Malden and Melrose, HUB MARK rubber footwear was sent to the far corners of the world.

Robinson Brothers & Company, manufacturers of toilet soap, was established in 1852 by Frederick R. Robinson. The business was owned by Roswell R. & Frederick A. Robinson in 1861. A new factory was erected in 1892 on Medford Street opposite the Bell Rock Cemetery. Potter Drug & Chemical Corporation took over the business and developed the well known Cuticura product known the world over

Original plant of the Boston Rubber Shoe Company in 1853.

since 1884. Several small concerns now occupy sections of the building.

Malden & Melrose Gas Light Company, incorporated in the spring of 1854, opened its first small office at 4 Florence Street with two employees. By 1900 it had over 90 miles of gas mains, supplying gas to Malden, Medford, Everett, and Melrose.

By 1847 Otis Tufts had built the first wharf at the old landing place at Sandy Bank. The Malden River had been dredged and straightened making it possible for barges to come up to deliver lumber, coal, and tar products. It was a common sight to see loaded barges plying the river to deliver cargoes to companies adjacent to the shore near Medford Street and beyond. This practice continued for years until the companies changed locations, closed, or used other means of transportation. The time-consuming process of raising the Medford Street drawbridge was not then an inconvenience to the horse-drawn mode of street travel. However, with the coming of the automobile and a faster pace demanded for all types of wheeled traffic, changes were necessary to update the narrow bridge for a quicker means of transportation.

Gould's Herb Factory, emitting a spicy, pungent odor for a considerable distance, stood on Main Street, near Winter Street, for years before it moved to the Forestdale section. The factory was a familiar spot in its earlier location.

There was a large blacksmith shop in this same neighborhood on

Entrance to Columbian Hall on Lebanon Street north of Maplewood Square just before the turn of the century. Photo courtesy of the Malden Evening News.

Winter Street. Its dark interior with its particular odor was lighted mostly by its flaming forge. The wide open doorway drew many a child and adult to watch the blacksmith as he plied his trade, the sparks flying high and increasing the excitement for the bystanders. This was but one of several such shops in Malden in the heyday of horses. They were busy places before the turn of the century, but with the coming of the automobile, the horse gradually was replaced by motorized vehicles. Nevertheless the horse continued to provide enjoyment for those who found horseback riding an exhilarating sport.

Not only did Malden flourish with new industries, but there was also an increase in civic development. In 1821 the first post office was located in Sargent's Block at the corner of Main and Ferry Streets, remaining there until 1830. It was moved to different locations, mostly along Pleasant Street, until a new structure was erected at the corner of Ferry and Prescott Streets. The latest move took place in 1966 when new quarters were opened on Mountain Avenue opposite Cotymore Lea.

The first street railway with horse-cars was built in Boston in 1836 and they appeared in Malden on July 19, 1858. The Middlesex Horse Railroad barn, built in 1863, was located at the corner of Abbott and Pleasant Streets about where the Strand Theatre stood

Pleasant Street from Central Square in 1867.

until it was demolished in 1973. Within this area were numerous livery stables, harness, and carriage shops. The horse-cars ran from Malden to Haymarket Square at a 10c fare! The first electric car was operated in Malden on January 13, 1894. The elevated service to Sullivan Square began on June 10, 1901. Between 1900-1915, in the exciting days of open-air trolleys with running boards built lengthwise to the seats, it was a thrilling experience for the "young fry" to take rides to West Medford or to Revere Beach. The clang of the motorman's bell as he stepped on it to clear the car track added to the excitement. The cars started at Florence Street and provided a ride the entire distance to the beach for ten cents.

In 1873 Malden could boast of 287 manufacturing firms, 20 shops, 6 churches, 1 bank, 6 hotels, and even 1 barber shop.

Fire Fighters

Malden had a band of volunteer fire fighters as early as 1820. That year a primitive kind of engine named the "Alert" was purchased by private funds for $437, but the ancient fire buckets were still kept in use. In 1819 a drive had been started to procure that hand-drawn fire engine. Over 100 citizens subscribed and the town's first regular fire engine was delivered on February 21, 1820. Fire Engine Co. 1 was formed and twenty-two men were appointed as "enginemen" by the selectmen. Malden's original engine house was located on the east side of Main Street, a short distance north of the First Baptist Church. On April 10, 1839, the selectmen were authorized to establish the Malden Fire Department by an act of the legislature. Five pieces of hand-drawn equipment were purchased up to 1854 with companies stationed in various sections of the town.

Until the fire station belfry had a bell the schoolhouse bell was rung for fire alarms. In 1864 the Central Fire Station located at 6 Pleasant Street, on the site of what is now the Dowling building, was built over the filled-in pond. It was a two-story wooden structure with a belfry which housed the bell operated by hand to sound alarms or to call the firemen together for their monthly meetings. That same year Malden purchased its first steamer, the *Wannalancet*.

The town made good use of deserted wooden schoolhouses. By 1864 Maplewood Fire quarters was located on Spruce Street. When the former Maplewood Schoolhouse moved to Laurel and Granite Streets in 1888, the old building was remodeled into a fire station. The brick firehouse at 4 Laurel Street was built in 1903 to replace the wooden one. Chemical No. 1 engine house was organized on Ashland Street in the wooden building formerly the Belmont Schoolhouse, after the new brick school was built in 1889. The brick station house was built in 1898 on the same lot. The Edgeworth Station at 176 Pearl Street opened its own brick building in 1891, moving three blocks from its original site at the corner of Pearl and Thacher Streets. The Ward 3 station in the West End, constructed at 22 Mountain Avenue opened late in 1896 but was closed in 1947 as a fire station. In 1898 a former wooden schoolhouse was remodeled in Linden for a second station in Ward 6, at the corner of Oliver and Clapp Streets. After the building was destroyed by fire on November 8, 1906, a brick firehouse was built the next year on the same site.

By 1873 fire equipment was completely horsedrawn. At this time the department consisted of 67 men with 4 fire companies. In 1875 a new fire station was built on Main Street on the site of a portion of Jordan Marsh Company and what later became the throughway of Exchange Street. This was the site where the First Church, Congregational, stood until destroyed by a tornado on September 19, 1869. The engine house was a three-door, two-story brick building with a high bell tower.

After Malden became a city, greater improvement brought the fire equipment up-to-date. Hydrants were erected and more firehouses were built. In 1900 Malden operated 10 fire companies from 6 different stations: Central, Station 1; Maplewood, Station 2; Edgeworth, Station 3; Ashland Street, Chemical 1; Mountain Avenue, Chemical 3; Linden, Station 4. By 1909 modernized pieces were purchased and with fire boxes erected around the city Malden was ready for emergencies. October, 1918, saw the last of the horses when all were retired or transferred to other city departments.

On April 1, 1919, the Main Street Central Station was abandoned and the department occupied the greatly enlarged and modern colonial brick building on Salem Street at the corner of Sprague Street. This was the first and only fire station built for motorized fire equipment in the city and continues to serve efficiently. Gradually, the department updated its equipment as new types of fire fighting apparatus were developed and money became available to purchase them.

Police Department

In March of 1874 many officials and citizens of Malden were concerned about the need for a police chief and a centrally located police station. By June a chief had been appointed by the selectmen, a set of rules and regulations had been adopted, and headquarters set up in the Town Hall. Some days later the department was officially organized with seven regular patrolmen and forty-nine special officers. The force was limited to three patrolmen doing night duty from 7 to 10 o'clock. A uniform for the officers was adopted and approved. Still visible in the basement of the Town Hall is a row of ten cells which comprised the ancient lockup.

In August, 1883, the city government moved police headquarters from the Town Hall to quarters over Murray & Wiley's Store, but by November, 1891, the police were back in City Hall. With a new office there, another innovation was introduced when a long distance telephone was installed, linking Malden with law enforcement agencies in distant cities as well as surrounding communities.

By 1906, plans were completed for a separate new building for police headquarters. The cornerstone was laid on August 18 that year, and the station at the corner of Middlesex and Exchange Streets was formally dedicated on March 25, 1907.

Many changes took place shortly after the turn of the century: Traffic became one of the busiest departments and continues to be so today. The department was modernized with Model T Fords, followed by the installation of two-way radios. In 1921 two Ford cars, an emergency wagon, and a motorcycle for a traffic officer were purchased by the city. A Liquor Squad and a Traffic Squad were definite requirements by the 1920's and necessitated an increase in personnel in both departments. With liquor licenses and liquor stores increasing in number, the Liquor Squad required that vigorous enforcement procedures be set up by the city government. In the late 1960's and early 1970's the drug problem became acute and the breakdown in morals added to the situation and continues to be a perplexing problem for city officials and various departments in these present vexatious times.

A Welcome Invention

On January 31, 1877, a quiet but remarkable demonstration which was to have far reaching results occurred at the home of Malden's Mayor, Elisha S. Converse. Over a private telephone wire which extended from the Congress Street (Boston) office of the Boston Rubber Shoe Company to the Edgeworth factory and from there to Mr. Converse's home on Main Street at the Malden-Everett line, Alexander Graham Bell demonstrated his newest invention, the box telephone. The Malden demonstration was the second of its kind to establish the commercial value of the telephone between distant points. By 1878 a crude switchboard was in operation and two years later the city learned it would "soon enjoy the convenience of telephonic communications with Boston."

Telephones quickly became a necessity in modern day life. On May 2, 1880, the Malden selectmen voted permission for the erection of telephone poles. At the turn of the century only 14 pay phone booths were scattered throughout Malden, but by 1935, there were 9,529 telephones in the city. Malden's first telephone exchange was established in 1881. On May 30, 1948, the Malden manual telephone system was changed to an automatic dial system, designed by Bell Telephone for the nearly 17,500 instruments in the city. The newly erected telephone building at 5 Elm Street has double the switching equipment to handle the greatly increased volume of calls.

Connections can now be made from Malden telephones to phones throughout the world as well as instruments installed in ships, trains, and automobiles. Global communication is commonplace thanks not only to underseas cables but also the three famous satellites, Echo, Telstar, and Syncom, which constantly circle the earth.

Development of Schooling After 1800

In 1849 Malden was divided into five school districts with ten teachers. After the founding of Malden High School in 1857, sessions were held in the original Centre Grammar School on Pleasant Street, about opposite Linden Avenue. Two years later, following the completion of the Town House, Malden's High School, with approximately sixty pupils, held its sessions in two rooms on the first floor of this town building. However, neither facilities proved satisfactory and such inadequate quarters brought about considerable agitation for a new building. Thus in 1872 the first separate high school building, of wooden construction, was built on Salem Street, about opposite Sprague Street. Sessions began with an enrollment of ninety-four pupils and four teachers. During the period when Charles A. Daniels was headmaster, the Malden High School Library was started with donations from the students, twenty years before the community had its public library.

The enrollment in the public schools totaled 2,106 in 1886 with an average of 44 pupils to a room, the Coverly School having just opened. Other schools were: High School, Centre, Maplewood, West, Judson, Emerson, Belmont, Greenwood, Linden, and Oak Grove. The Evening School had been operating in two sections of the city for the past 3 years with an attendance of 131, 83 students being in the Evening Drawing School. The average annual per pupil cost had increased from $8.69 in 1863 to $28.47 in 1885.

After the student body exceeded five hundred by 1896, the city built another high school building which opened in 1899, this of red brick construction, also on Salem Street adjacent to the wooden structure. The older building became the Manual Arts building. In 1907 this was moved to an adjoining lot and housed the offices of the superintendent and truant officer. It was occupied until 1938 when it was torn down.

After 1890 five schools were constructed; Ayers, Faulkner, Lincoln, Linden and Glenwood. In 1905 Browne was built and in 1906 the Daniels was constructed. The first school building in Malden was erected by public funds. It served to promote elementary school edu-

The Wooden High School built in 1872 on Salem Street, from a photo taken in the early nineteen hundreds.

cation. The Lincoln and Browne Junior High Schools were opened in 1925, the Beebe Junior High in 1928. Three new schools were constructed after 1934 with additions to five others. The new buildings included: Emerson, 1939; Linden, 1953; Forestdale, 1956. There were additions to Malden High, 1939; Lincoln Junior, 1939 and again in 1958. New sections were added to Belmont in 1939 and Daniels in 1958. With these additions the archaic wooden school buildings of the Franklin, Judson, Converse and Ayers were eliminated. A Linden school wing was destroyed by fire in March, 1956.

Progress in the school system was apparent. In 1912, high school semi-annual promotions in January and June were instituted but were discontinued in 1934 when the disadvantages far outweighed the advantages. Afternoon sessions for high school students were begun after World War I. Enrollment rose sharply as students lost their wartime jobs, nevertheless a great number of young people were reluctant to return to school since their wartime jobs had paid as high as $14.00 per week.

By 1923 the ninth grade was eliminated from grade schools. That same year, a dental clinic was set up. The Schick Test for school children was started about 1924, and the High School Band was first organized with both boys and girls participating. Its purpose was to

Captain William Winship, Malden's "historian" of his day, musters the High School Cadets on Decoration Day, 1886.

further interest in music among the students and provide added stimulation for participation in school games, parades, and other civic events.

Growth in enrollment made it necessary by 1928 to use the Centre Grammar School on Ferry Street, built in 1875, as an annex for high school classes. Crossing Ferry Street from the main building to the annex became a hazard but conditions were endured until 1940 without serious incidents. After the addition of an east wing in 1908, to correspond with the west wing, the center section of the red brick High School was renovated. An impressive center entrance with the city seal carved high above the entrance added a significant historical emblem to the facade.

A campaign was begun for a new high school annex or an addition. Time and again a new school was proposed, and each proposal met rejection by the city government. By 1936 Malden's Mayor John D. Devir suggested construction of a new building with the aid of a Public Works Administration (P.W.A.) grant covering forty-five percent of the cost. With the city government approval in April and a federal grant in August of the next year, work soon got underway with the razing of the Manual Arts building, razing of houses on Berkeley Street, Holden Street west side and the permanent closing of Berkeley Street.

On December 12, 1939, the new High School, built of buff brick, was declared ready for occupancy. On the 19th the new addition opened with seventeen hundred students enrolled. Immediately after the transition was made from the old quarters to the new, work was started on the remodeling of the older building.

Students in all of Malden's schools shared in World War II efforts during 1941-45. Many of legal age entered military service. Others studied first aid, rolled bandages, and gave clerical assistance wherever needed. Some were attracted to part-time jobs in wartime industries with the largest salaries ever paid. It was then that "CHAW" (Christmas At Work) came into being. Teachers were involved along with students. Rationing and daily routine were upsetting people's lives. "Black-outs" became accepted. High school schedules as well as family life were upset by wartime employment.

In 1957 the high school had a year-long celebration to commemorate the centennial of the founding of the school. Three junior high schools, ten elementary schools, an evening school and home instruction program, comprised the system. The high school driver training course started in 1952 and grew rapidly with the addition of a control Ford supplied by a local firm.

Three Roman Catholic Parochial Schools operated by the three Catholic churches provided education for Catholic young people. Girls' Catholic High was founded in 1908 by the pastor of the Church of the Immaculate Conception. In 1923 the students moved to their new building on the West Street side of the school yard. The new high school building was begun in 1922.

In 1969 the population stood at 58,213 with 27,266 enrolled voters. Enrollment in Malden's public schools that year exceeded 10,000 with 10,203 students attending the 15 schools in the system. A senior high, vocational, three junior highs, and ten elementary schools and several special classes comprised the educational program in the city. The school system pioneered in the establishment of classes for the mentally retarded and emotionally disturbed and also was among the first to introduce a "learning disability class" for children who experienced difficulty in communicating. A teacher for non-English speaking children provided special instruction for the city's twenty-six children in this category. Supplementing the regular school program, an evening school continues to offer adult education to those who enroll for the winter sessions.

200th Anniversary

In 1849 the 200th Anniversary of the town was celebrated on May 23rd with an oration by James D. Green, son of one of Malden's founders, and a lengthy original poem written and delivered by Gilbert Haven, Jr. The town published the *Bi-Centennial Book of Malden* in 1850 covering the proceedings of the observance and included genealogies of some of Malden's old families. The Ancient Ministry of Malden, religious societies, historical items, and a summary of such miscellaneous matters as education, population, taxation, roads and bridges, military matters, town officers and manners and customs, make this book a most useful addition to the town's history.

Cemeteries

Space in the ancient burial place at Sandy Bank, later named Bell Rock, containing 3.3 acres, became scarce in the early 1820's. Consequently, in 1828 there was established in the northern part of the town the "North Burying Ground," later known as "The Village Cemetery" of Melrose after 1850. This "Village Burying Ground" was completely vacated by the end of 1896 with removal of those interred to the newer cemetery. Land for Wyoming Cemetery was bought from the farmland of Joseph Lynde on Main Street and Charles Pratt on Lebanon Street in Melrose. Wyoming Cemetery was dedicated in July, 1857.

After 1832 "Sandy Bank" was known as "The Old Burying Ground," and about 1882 it was called "Bell Rock Cemetery" due entirely to the interest of Malden's eminent historian, Deloraine P. Corey. Records between 1640 and 1649, when no doubt many deaths occurred among the very early settlers on Mystic Side, are lost. The earliest of these records list Margaret Lewis, wife of John Lewis. She died April 10, 1649, he died in September, 1657, and both, no doubt, were buried at Sandy Bank. The gravestone of Alice Brackenbury, wife of William, dated December 28, 1670, bears the earliest date in the burying ground. County records list the deaths of 51 persons before that of Alice Brackenbury and up to November, 1699, a total of 148 were listed as having died in Malden, and probably were buried in Sandy Bank. A few of those buried there were moved to the Salem Street Buying Ground after it was opened, and in 1899 eight Sprague gravestones were moved to Forest Dale Cemetery.

There are three other cemeteries, set apart years ago within the boundaries of the city. They include the extensive area of Holy Cross

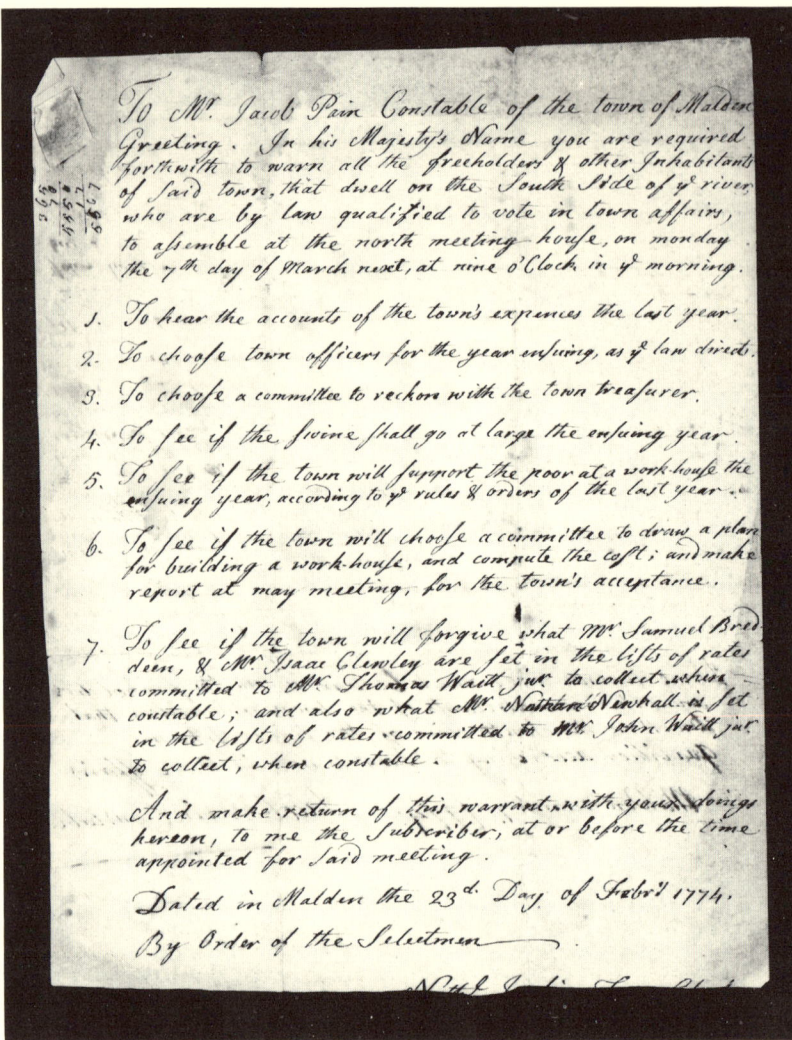

Warrant for a Town Meeting, dated February 23, 1774. The seven articles listed for consideration all concern routine town business, in marked contrast to the warrant of May 21, 1776 on page 108.

on Broadway and St. Mary's on Fellsway East, bounded by Savin and Pine Streets, both owned by the Archdiocese of Boston, and the small Jewish plot on Lebanon Street near Sylvan Street, under the care of Malden Post, Jewish War Veterans.

Heritage of Bell Rock Cemetery

Five craftsmen are definitely known who carved many of the designs and epitaphs in Malden's oldest burying ground, making this hallowed acreage one of the finest in all New England. Here can be found the earliest examples of American sculpture.

One early gravestone bears the name of Marcy Allin who died in 1678. The one and only ornamentation carved on her stone resembles a rosette. This design is an exact duplicate of one in the oldest burying ground in Cambridge, the only two with this rosette still standing in any burying ground. They were carved by one of the earliest and most prominent, as well as reputable such craftsmen in the colony. He was known simply as The Stone Cutter of Boston, his name never revealed or recorded for posterity.

Many stones were cut by Joseph Lamson who became a Malden resident and was active in town affairs. He married Elizabeth Mitchell in 1679. He carved her stone after her death in 1703 and that of their daughter who died in 1704, aged 14 years. His two sons, Nathaniel and Caleb, were both popular stonecutters and some of their work can be seen in Bell Rock. The Lamsons had almost a stonecutting monopoly in Middlesex County. They developed definite designs carved only by them and these became their trade mark. James Foster of Dorchester is another craftsman whose work is seen and who developed his own trade mark. He married Anna, daughter of Job Lane, who built Malden's 1658 meeting house. Foster cut both Job Lane's stone and that of his wife.

Moving a coffin to Sandy Bank (Bell Rock) Burying Ground before wheeled vehicles became common was not an easy task, especially from outlying sections of the town. It often required sixteen bearers who carried the coffin all the way on their shoulders, with the mourners trudging behind. One historical chronicler remarked that "wine and rum were as necessary to bury a pauper as a prince."

In April, 1832, a committee of three was appointed at Town Meeting to purchase a portion of land on Salem Street suitable for a "New Burial Ground." Additional land purchases were made in 1864 and again in 1867 to the extent of 4.5 acres, the area being designated as "Salem Street Cemetery." The earliest date on a gravestone here records Mary Alice Pickering, October 4, 1832. In May, 1937, the present wall 355 feet long was built by W.P.A. workmen. The gate was designed and constructed by the firm of Babcock Davis Co., and installed the same year.

The land included within the grounds of Forest Dale Cemetery which contains fifty-six acres was first allotted to Thomas Lynde in the great allotment of lands in 1638-39 by Charlestown authorities. The present home of the Superintendent of Cemeteries now stands on the very spot where Thomas Lynde built his farmhouse before 1653. (It was John Pratt who tore down the old Thomas Lynde house and built the present brick-end house in 1830.) This tract of land remained in the Lynde family until 1753, after which it was sold and at least six other owners acquired it at various times. By 1883 the land had been purchased by the city, and an additional five acres were purchased in 1899 making a total of sixty-one acres within the bounds of the cemetery. The first interments were on June 29, 1885, when James O'Brien and his children were buried. The cemetery was dedicated on Memorial Day, May 30, 1885, with impressive services. More and more vacant areas within the stonewall cemetery are continually being prepared for burials.

Maplewood

The area east of the center of Malden developed slowly. It was first called Scadan. A schoolhouse, painted yellow, was built in 1771 to meet the requirements of the law, the first public building in that section. By 1807 there were at least ten houses in various clearings. From then on the area developed over the ensuing years. The greatest advancement was encouraged when Joshua Webster came from Lynn in 1851 and purchased portions of the old Waite farm. He developed that section, laid out streets and house lots, and with the planting of a large number of maple trees the area lost the name Scadan and thereafter was known as Maplewood. The bell which had hung in the cupola in the 1858 wooden Maplewood schoolhouse and had called the school children to classes, was given to St. Joseph's Parish at the time the schoolhouse was torn down in 1886. The bell was later hung in the Chapel belfry in Holy Cross Cemetery. In 1883 a stage coach line was operating in Maplewood and three years later horse-cars were traveling down the Salem Road. These were followed by the electric railway and then jitneys.* Next, larger and more modern buses ran through the main street by 1930 replacing the street cars. Maplewood had its own theatre with movies for all ages to enjoy.

Other sections of Malden gradually developed covering Linden, Faulkner, Oak Grove, the West End, Edgeworth, Belmont Hill and Forestdale. All grew into sectional communities long before buses made traveling easier from each of these sections to Malden Center.

Separation of Melrose

After the Boston & Maine Railroad began operations in July, 1845, more families settled in North Malden or the "Village." The population was somewhat depleted in Malden by the separation of Melrose in 1850. As the activities there were so distinct from those in the center of Malden, the residents petitioned the General Court for incorporation as a town, and with the support of the Malden voters this was accomplished. The Town of Melrose was incorporated May 3, 1850, with a population of about 1,260.

The Town Hall

In 1857 the town of Malden purchased for $5,000 the land where Hill's Tavern or "The Rising Eagle" stood for the erection of a Town Hall. Originally built by Moses Hill in 1725, it had served the town well. The tavern was moved to the corner of Main and Irving Streets where it was occupied until November of 1914. Jonathan Clark, a carpenter, who had come to Malden from Wells, Maine, and built his house on Wyoming Avenue (still standing), was given the contract to build the building in accordance with plans drawn up by John Stevens of Boston.

The dedication was held on October 29, that same year of 1857, with quite a detailed program. Originally the building was designed with two circular stairways leading directly to a large hall capable of holding a thousand persons. A second smaller hall was built on the third or top floor. The building was gas lighted and heated by two furnaces on the main floor. Phineas Sprague and James Pierce each ran a dry goods store on the first floor. A high school with thirty-eight pupils was started in the building and continued there until 1871

---

*Very small buses, actually five-passenger Ford touring cars were used in Malden at one time.

Malden City Hall decorated for the 250th Anniversary celebration in May of 1899.

when a three-story wooden building was erected at the corner of Salem and Berkeley Streets. During the years the high school was in the Town Hall school work exhibitions were displayed when graduation exercises were held there. The Town House was the second brick building in the growing town, the earlier one (known as the Waite Block and diagonally opposite in the Square) was built in the early 1850's by Deacon Thomas Waite, and is standing today. The passageway next to the Main Street Town Hall was part of the sale of land to the city. "Together with the $5,000 land sale, Mrs. Hill and heirs were granted a 17 foot right-of-way leading to their personal property." That right-of-way has become a foot path and driveway of late years. The Town Hall was completed at a cost of $24,998.30.

The second floor was used by numerous organizations including the Edgeworth School and Engine Co. 2. From 1857 to July 1, 1868,

Mount Vernon Lodge of Masons rented space. Murray & Wiley's gentlemen's furnishings hired quarters in the building. On February 14, 1879, Malden's first public library opened on the first floor and remained there until the new library building was ready for occupancy. The police occupied a room until new quarters were built for the department on Middlesex Street. "In 1860, the Malden Lyceum met in the large hall and well known speakers including Charles Sumner, Wendell Phillips, the Rev. Edward Everett Hale, all leading reformers and abolitionists, delivered addresses."

By 1883, the Town House was officially known as the City Hall. "Mayor John K.C. Sleeper was the first official to occupy an office with chambers designated for councilmen and aldermen as well as Assessors."

Fellsmere Pond

This attractive pond in its wooded setting along Fellsway East, below Malden Hospital, was made possible from a bequest by the Honorable John K.C. Sleeper, Malden's second mayor.

The Civil War

In 1861 the country was in the throes of the Civil War. At the time of its outbreak Malden's population numbered about 6,000 persons. Military requirements were met when the need arose and the names of 807 men were listed as serving in the army or navy during the succeeding years of strife. Twenty-three were killed or died of their wounds; fifteen died in Confederate prisons; twenty-eight died from diseases while in the service. Malden's first Civil War casualty was Gordon Forrest, Sergeant, aged thirty-one, killed at Blackburn's Ford, Virginia, on Bull Run, July 18, 1861.

Some women took in government work at home using sewing machines which had just come into popular use. Others sold bonds or used their linens to make bandages for the wounded. Malden Ladies Soldiers' Aid Society was organized, October 11, 1861, "to afford relief to our soldiers and especially to the sick and wounded through the Sanitary Commission," as the purpose of the Society stated. Starting with fifty-two members, its membership increased to one hundred its second year, but by April, 1865, people had become war-weary with hopes of peace in prospect and the society disbanded. While active, meetings were held in the high school room of the Town Hall where

Growth

boxes were packed for the Commission with clothing, bedding, hospital supplies, dried fruit, and jellies. A two-day successful festival held in the Town Hall in February, 1862, and a concert given by school children, July 9, 1863, netted substantial income for the women's work.

Civil War tablets on the monument at Bell Rock Park list those who served in the war from Malden.

Women's Advancement

By an Act of the Legislature women were declared eligible to serve as members of the School Committee in 1874. It took another Act of the Legislature in 1879 to give women the right to vote for School Committee members. In 1881 Malden granted women the authority to vote for members of that committee. Mrs. Harriette Robinson Shattuck, a pioneer in many fields for the advancement of women as well as an outstanding leader in the suffrage movement and founder of Old and New, the earliest women's club of Malden, was the first woman in the state to be registered to vote for the School Committee and she paid $2.00 for the privilege.

Pure Water Supply

Water was first piped from Spot Pond in 1870 by a system later absorbed by the Metropolitan Water Commission. Spot Pond, partly in Stoneham and partly in Medford in the Middlesex Fells Reservation, was first mentioned in the journal of Governor John Winthrop in 1632. He and a few of his followers came upon it on February 7th of that year and named it "Spots Pond" in recognition of the rocky islets that spotted its surface. Although known for the purity of its water, nothing was done to secure control of the supply until 1867 when it was incorporated as the Spot Pond Water Company by residents of the three towns of Malden, Medford and Melrose. Pipes were laid after the franchise was purchased by the towns in 1869, and water became available for the towns in 1870. A 16-inch pump was installed in 1881. Occasional drought threatened the water supply and by the end of 1885 land for a reservoir on Fairmount Hill had been purchased and a pumping station installed. On January 1, 1898, following an Act of the General Court, control of the Spot Pond water supply passed into the hands of the Metropolitan District Commission. Spot Pond has a 2 billion gallon capacity and has water piped in from Quabbin Reservoir, the main reservoir serving some 1.7 million persons in 33 Greater Boston communities. On January 5, 1975, the Spot Pond pumping station was damaged by fire.

Everett Separation

The incorporation of Everett in 1870 marked the beginning of a separate municipality which continued to grow over the years. Manufacturing became a major industry, with many large plants contributing to the prosperity of the developing city.

Organizations

THE WOMEN'S CHRISTIAN TEMPERANCE UNION was organized in 1874 and continued well into the present century, actively programmed with earnest devotion by those who promoted its activities. It was a leading group in social reform. Malden's branch gave considerable assistance with its concern for community problems which the members of the organization labored to improve. By the 1950's the leading workers, because of advancing age and failing health, were forced to retire. New members were not forthcoming so gradually the work of the Union faded.

The modest beginning of the MALDEN PUBLIC LIBRARY which resulted from some three years of public demand was brought about largely through the efforts of the Young Men's Deliberative Assembly.

After two unsuccessful attempts, one in 1871 and another in 1876, the Malden Public Library was established on March 12, 1877, with a bequest of $5,000 from a former resident, John Gardner. Subsequently a Board of Trustees numbering eleven was elected by ballot at Town Meeting. The library was first opened for the public's use on February 14, 1879, and housed in the quarters of the later City Treasurer's office in the Town Hall. The library had a collection of 3,643 volumes which had been carefully selected by the trustees. With additional volumes and an increase in the number of people using the facilities, another building appeared imperative. A gift was made to the city of the handsome Converse Memorial Building on October 1, 1885, by the Honorable Elisha S. Converse and his wife, Mary D. Converse, as a memorial to their son, Frank Eugene Converse, who had died in 1863. With the many works of art and furnishings donated by them this building became a prominent landmark. Built of brown sandstone and designed by the leading American architect of the period, Henry Hobson Richardson, in his well-known Romanesque style, it served adequately for a time. Two wings were added in 1897 for book stacks, a reading and reference room, and an art gallery. The octagonal Children's Room (then so designated) and the Ryder Gallery above it were not added until 1915. The iron gates at the main entrance on Salem Street were erected in 1911 in memory of Lillie A. B. Hill from the proceeds of a gift received from her in 1910.

During 1921 a generous contributor to the Library, Roswell R. Robinson left $10,000 for free lectures. With the income from this fund and an annual gift of $400 for several years from his daughter, Helen Robinson Richards, the proceeds provided funding for the popular winter lectures which have continued since their inception. Additional grants have been donated from the Davenport Memorial Foundation and a $10,000 contribution anonymously donated during the 1950's by Miss Ena L. Metcalf with an additional sum of $20,000 left by her upon her death, October 1, 1974, at the advanced age of 102 years.

In 1886 the MALDEN HISTORICAL SOCIETY was formally organized during March by twelve founders. The Honorable Elisha S. Converse was elected its first president. In 1898 many changes were made in the bylaws. Four meetings were held yearly in place of monthly meetings; the acquisition of historical relics relating to Malden was authorized; and on May 2nd thirteen women were elected to membership for the first time. Among the fourteen presidents to date two have been women: Mrs. Walton S. Hall and Miss Dorothy L. Rothe.

The MALDEN YMCA was established in 1859 when the building was erected on Pleasant Street, corner of Linden Avenue. Ground breaking took place in February of 1859, the laying of the cornerstone on May 18th that same year. The "Y" has been a helpful and comfortable home for many men and the addition of a gym was of great value for groups and individuals. Since the latest exterior reconstruction, completed in 1974, the building presents a fine appearance and fills a real community need.

Assistance from women was enlisted even before the building was built. In September of 1886 a Ladies Aid Committee was formed to raise money for the new "Y" and its furnishings. On October 17, 1888, a Woman's Auxiliary was organized to conform with the newly organized groups in other cities and states with representation from each Protestant church in the locality where a "Y" was established. By

Main hall of Malden Public Library, designed in the classic Romanesque style of the well-known library architect, Henry Hobson Richardson.

the time ground breaking took place the auxiliary had a membership of over five hundred women. By means of various earlier projects and one huge bazaar held in the new building for a week during December, 1895, the auxiliary assumed the financial burden of furnishing the entire quarters, except the section set up for physical activities. The women also were responsible for the housekeeping and overseeing the comfort of the residents. The women's role continued for some time until the "Y" no longer had need of their services in these capacities.

On September 16, 1891, a group of Malden citizens and businessmen who had faith in the future of the city, formed a corporation under the name of the MALDEN BOARD OF TRADE. Because its scope of activity had broadened to encompass every phase of industrial, commercial, and civic responsibility, in January, 1921, the Malden Board of Trade petitioned the Commonwealth of Massachusetts to change its name to the MALDEN CHAMBER OF COMMERCE. This civic-minded organization still functions effectively with headquarters on Dartmouth Street, conveniently close to Malden Square.

The MALDEN DELIBERATIVE ASSEMBLY, a live-wire organization, was founded in 1875.

Another forward step in the development of the city was the establishment of a city park system in 1892.

MALDEN HIGH SCHOOL held military drills in the 1800's, its football and baseball teams playing their games first at Bruce's Field and later at Ferryway Green before a permanent stadium was built.

MALDEN HOSPITAL A long awaited addition to the needs of the city and its people was welcomed when on July 7, 1892, Malden Hospital opened its doors on Hospital Hill with thirty-eight beds in three wards and eight private rooms. A horse-drawn ambulance transported patients. The hospital was used only for emergencies, sick people being cared for in the homes where they were born and usually died. Although the cornerstone was laid in 1890, the hospital's first patient was not admitted until 1892. The discovery of the X-ray in the last decade of the 19th century introduced a new era of costly equipment for use in the medical field. Malden civic leaders were equal to the challenge and Malden Hospital continues to be proud of its standing in the community and the state.

The principal benefactor and leading force in the effort to establish a hospital in Malden was the Honorable Elisha S. Converse. It was he who, in 1890, called a meeting at his home of a group of civic-minded men, including several doctors. Mr. Converse donated a tract of land for the hospital building. A corporation was formed, a building fund drive organized, and an architect employed. Shortly after the hospital opened a School of Nursing was organized with five students entering the first class.

One of the doctors of the city was concerned about the need for financing the hospital and he transmitted this concern to Mr. Converse. It was First Church, Congregational, that first heard about this doctor's objective. Since he was a member, he approached the church authorities to lay his idea before them. At a church meeting held on November 3, 1890, it was voted "that the Church Committee fix some Sunday convenient for all churches in the city to observe Hospital Sunday, the offering to be devoted to the proposed Malden Hospital by passing the boxes." Subsequently the churches in the community observed the first "Hospital Sunday" on January 18, 1891, when the united offerings were contributed to the hospital fund. Dr. Andrew J. Stevens, a city physician, was this First Church member who sponsored the action and sparked the "Hospital Sunday" project. On his gravestone in Forest Dale Cemetery is carved this tribute: "Through his influence and efforts the Malden Hospital was established." His initial idea and his deep concern carried great influence in initiating this special church observance. This annual "Hospital Sunday" offering was held for forty years, adding great financial encouragement when the hospital was growing and developing its program of service.

Around the turn of the century a log cabin was built and equipped for convalescent patients and a cottage previously used for patients with contagious diseases was converted into a maternity ward. In 1906, through the financial efforts of the Ladies' Aid Association, a building was constructed to house a children's ward. A new surgical unit building was started in 1922 and that year two thousand patients were admitted to the hospital. Through several building fund drives wings were added to the main hospital, and the latest equipment was purchased to keep abreast of modern medical methods. A skilled and qualified medical and nursing staff serves the institution, as well as competent housekeeping personnel, directed by an efficient administrative staff.

A greatly enlarged building covers an extensive area on Hospital Hill. This accredited hospital at the present time (1975) has a patient capacity of 292 beds with a section readied for the new born arrivals of forty-seven bassinets. A new School of Nursing building, opened in the fall of 1970, was built below the main hospital. The earlier Nurses Home adjacent to the power plant was torn down in 1973. In the fall of 1973 fifty-six freshmen students, including both women and men, were enrolled in the largest class in the history of the 81-year-old Malden Hospital School of Nursing. Recent expansion and physical interior construction have been accomplished to bring the hospital up to the full accreditation requirements, upholding its customary high standards.

MAIN STREET MATERNITY HOSPITAL Although a house had been purchased in 1900 to serve as a maternity ward, it only provided quarters for twelve patients. With more prospective mothers desiring hospital care, these facilities proved inadequate before too long. By March of 1912 a canvass of the city was made and community fund-raising projects on a large scale were undertaken to accumulate money for a new Maternity Hospital.

In 1917 a substantial and timely gift became a real blessing to the community when Mr. and Mrs. Costello C. Converse donated the Colonel Harry E. Converse estate (at the corner of Appleton and Main Streets, where The Church of God now stands) to the city for the much needed hospital. The estate contained a forty-room house, a stable, garage, and extensive grounds.

The Ladies' Aid Association undertook the refurbishing of the house for hospital quarters and transformed the stable into a nurses' home. The formal opening took place on June 6, 1918, and the quarters were officially closed on December 31, 1932. During the thirteen and a half years this Maternity Hospital functioned on Main Street, 5,835 babies were born there.

THE LADIES' AID ASSOCIATION OF THE MALDEN HOSPITAL The association was formed February 17, 1892, by a group of women representing the churches of Malden. Its purpose was to assist in financial and other ways to benefit the hospital. During its long years of existence there have been but few projects; however, each one has been of profitable and lengthy duration. Besides three week-long Carnivals in the early days, Harvest Sales were held for thirty-seven years; the Penny Wise Trading Post conducted a brisk business for seventeen years; and there was a Cook Book Sale that brought fine financial rewards. Since 1956 the Coffee-Gift Shoppe at the hospital has been the major project with generous proceeds being contributed to the hospital each June for the purchase of definite pieces of equipment, and large donations being made toward building construction as well as yearly gifts being offered for student nurses' scholarships. Its membership of more than three hundred continues to contribute volunteer hours in the two shoppes and to increase the usefulness of the association for the welfare of the hospital.

JUNIOR HOSPITAL AID was organized during October of 1912 by thirteen young women and the membership increased to fifty by the end of the following year. This younger group of women also contributes funds to the hospital, the Children's Ward receiving their financial support. Various projects including an annual ball held for many years help to increase the group's financial donations to the hospital.

CONTAGIOUS HOSPITAL After an epidemic of smallpox, and in an effort to protect the city from the spreading of dangerous contagious diseases, land was purchased and a small building erected for

Residence of Benjamin F. Dutton, Glen Rock, in 1899.

a Contagious Hospital with accommodations for about fifteen patients. This type of hospital was maintained by the city on Forest Street beyond Forest Dale Cemetery until it was no longer needed.

Prosperity Leads to Maturity

The devotion of Mr. Converse to his adopted town of Malden was largely instrumental in securing its incorporation. In the year 1880 many of the leading citizens began to consider the advisability of establishing a city form of government in place of the town meeting, as soon as the population should reach the requisite number of twelve thousand. At a Town Meeting held in the Town Hall on November 23, 1880, it was voted to apply to the state legislature for a city charter. After receiving the town's petition the legislature passed an act, approved March 31, 1881, for the establishment of the City of Malden. The original charter provided for the election of a mayor, one alderman and three common councilmen chosen from each of the six wards; a seventh ward was added in 1889. Malden citizens voted to accept the charter on June 9th that same year and the election of the necessary officers was held on December 6th. The charter further provided, among several other items, for the election of a nine member school committee board, however, by legislative act approved in 1908, the school board was reduced to five members as it is at the present time. The new government was inaugurated on January 2, 1882, in the Common Council Chamber of Town Hall with Elisha S. Converse as Malden's first Mayor, having been elected by an almost unanimous vote.

Gradually a city began to emerge from the quiet country town founded by the first settlers over two hundred years earlier. The population increased and with it came the need for more and better housing, educational facilities and municipal services. The rapid growth of the city resulted in the building of many fine homes, and soon the population had reached 16,470 inhabitants.

By 1886 Malden had been in operation as a city for only four years and the city fathers faced many difficult decisions. There was the problem of financing new street development. There was a health menace caused by the absence of a sewerage system. The lack of sufficient water from Spot Pond to supply residents of Medford, Melrose, and Malden, had become acute and a remedy was vital for these growing communities. Most important of all was the need for additional financial revenues to help pay for these and other improvements. They solved the problem by adopting two laws, one approving a poll tax, the other providing for a new method of assessing taxes on real estate. The lack of a sewerage system had become extremely serious, and finally the erection of wooden buildings in addition to those already in existence in Malden Center emphasized the need for a building inspector and regulations to reduce fire hazards.

By 1892 Malden had reached the height of its public transportation service with its horse-cars, about a dozen daily trains on the Saugus Branch, and as many as sixty-six passenger trains on the Boston and Maine's western division, all of which provided daily service for the area's three thousand commuters. Stage coach and private horse-drawn vehicles had been earlier methods of transportation to Boston. Late in the 1920's the "gas buggy" offered a more luxurious method of travel along with the trolley car, train and bus. Public transportation systems had been the only means of travel until the automobile became popular and soon cars and commercial vehicles began to clog the main highways.

There were six stations in Malden on the Saugus Branch: Bell

Traffic jam at Broadway and Howard Street in Everett, 1897. Photo courtesy Anthony F. Tieuli.

Rock, Ferry Street, Faulkner, Maplewood, Broadway and Linden, the latter depot having been made famous by Eliot Paul's best seller, *Linden on the Saugus Branch*. The Boston & Maine steam trains crossed Pleasant Street at a busy grade crossing in the early years, about where the overpass at Pleasant and Summer Streets is today. The brick Summer Street depot (now a banquet hall) was built in 1892 after several bad accidents occurred at the lower street crossing. All of the Saugus Branch stations are gone and most of the stations on the Boston to Lowell route of the railroad have not survived.

The yellow trolleys of the Eastern Massachusetts line were familiar means of travel for awhile, a car barn standing where the Robin Hood Motel is now located at Broadway Square in Maplewood. This was the location of one of Malden's first traffic lights, a forerunner of today's seemingly countless red and green sentinels. The Eastern Massachusetts trolley line discontinued service in the 1920's after which buses provided the necessary service. Plans have been in the formative stage for some years now for "rapid transit" rail service along the old Boston & Maine Railroad route running as far as the Melrose line.

Electricity came to Malden on July 1, 1886. The generating equipment, office, and three-man personnel were housed in a small wooden structure. Original contracts for lighting twenty-three arc lamps for eighteen customers were secured. In September the city

Growth

Malden in 1837, from an old woodcut. The tin shops of Timothy Bailey and James H. Putnam and the law office of Charles Lewis are all included in this early view.

contracted for six street lamps to be lighted from dusk to midnight. Incandescent lamplighting for stores and homes became available during January of 1887 at a cost of $1.00 a month per lamp. In September, 1890, the company announced all-night electric service for its customers.

Business Enterprises

In 1898 the population stood at 32,051, at the height of the city's prosperity with growing numbers of industries, schools, organizations, and churches. Among developing firms the following could be counted:

PRESCOTT & SON, an insurance firm was established in 1855 and carried on by four succeeding generations of the family until 1968.

Samuel Cox had established a shoe last business in 1812, making the first last cut with a jackknife. Under the direction of his son, George Parker Cox, the last factory became the oldest established firm in Malden as late as 1899.

JAMES HUGGINS & SON, manufacturers of coal tar products, had started an enterprising business as early as 1862.

E. D. KAULBACK & SON opened a florist business in 1870 with greenhouses located off Highland Avenue and a shop on Pleasant Street.

A. N. WARD & SON, successor to Rogers Funeral Service on Maple Street, first offered services to Malden people in 1872.

CHARLES W. HOWARD & SON in 1882 and E. A. STEVENS & CO. soon thereafter became well known as Malden realtors.

LEWIS CANDY COMPANY opened quarters in 1883 and its product became well known over the years.

MORGAN'S PHARMACY, which conducted its business for more than sixty years on Pleasant Street, opened in 1884. Five years later, HUNT'S DRUG STORE opened on Main Street, Malden Square, and continues in business at 500 Main Street.

CLIFFORD-BLACK & CO. opened in 1889 with home furnishings.

In 1891 JOSLIN'S, Malden's first complete household goods and clothing store, opened and soon became the foremost store in the city for the next fifty years. Except for a few small stores along Pleasant Street, Joslin's covered the entire block.

ALFRED L. JACOBSON, INC., builders, began business in 1895.

In 1889 the FAMILY LAUNDRY COMPANY opened and prospered in its humble beginnings on Eastern Avenue, moving later to a modern brick structure on Dartmouth Street. With the introduction of coin-operated washing and drying machines providing cheaper conveniences for the family, the owners of the once profitable Family Laundry closed the Malden plant.

"Charles Niedner's Sons Company at 10 James Street opened for business in 1892. The company and factory were sold on August 6, 1969, since the area was needed for lower income apartments. The business moved to 65 Clinton Street in smaller quarters where it continues to carry on the Niedner operation. The factory in Coaticook, Canada, is still in operation. This firm has always been the leading manufacturer of linen fire hose and today is one of the few producers of linen hose in this country."

There were a number of newspapers published in the city at one period or another. The only one still existing with wide distribution is the *Malden Evening News,* established in 1892 with early quarters on Main Street in Malden Square. Other publications are listed here with approximate dates: *Malden Messenger,* (1856-1872); *Malden Mirror,* (1870-1914); *Malden Tribune,* (1872-1875); *Malden City Press,* (1880-1895); *Malden Evening Mail,* (1887-1919); *Malden Free Press,* (1914-1921, 1934-1959); *Malden Telegram,* (1921-1922).

Barrett's Opera House on Main Street, where Kotzen's Furniture Store was later built, was the site of numerous fairs, rallies, lectures, and for awhile, religious services.

Development of Sports and Arts

A croquet and bicycle craze swept the nation in 1892 and Malden residents also succumbed to the fads. Both forms of exercise were popular for many years and highlighted "The Gay Nineties" of the 1890's and early 1900's. Croquet and cycling appealed to the female sex but immediately both were condemned as women's sports because they exposed feminine ankles. Nevertheless the enthusiasm for both activities continued unabated.

In the early 1970's bicycle riding became extremely popular among children and adults and the popular sport has far outstripped the earlier interest with both young people and adults finding pleasure in the high speed two-wheelers. Tennis has also grown into a competitive sport and vies with many other professional games, gaining popularity each succeeding year. The attraction for sports has been heightened since the various types of games have been featured on television in greater numbers during the 1972-1973 seasons, professional sports having become big business.

Baseball, already popular before the Civil War, began to emerge by 1892 as a national pastime. Football gained in popularity from its inception in 1889 when Walter C. Camp chose his first "All American" team. Basketball, invented in 1891 by James Naismith, a Y.M.C.A. instructor in Springfield, became an indoor winter sport which gained interest among boys of high school age.

Enjoyment of music was heightened with the invention of the phonograph. It delighted those who, by the 1900's, owned one or could listen to the shrill records. Probably the memory of the familiar dog cocking an ear to the sound coming from the horn-type phonograph "box" traces back to the earliest machine.

The Civil War gave a monumental lift to the budding art of photography. Every mother wanted a picture of her son in uniform and more realistic photographs of family members became the rage. They replaced the tintype and daguerreotype pictures to be found among the Victorian era parlor knick-knacks, along with a stereopticon viewer and its photographic slides. This was a favorite parlor pastime beginning about 1850 when the three-dimensional stereoscopic pictures thrilled many a child as well as adult. The hand stereoscope, still collectable, was invented in 1859 by Oliver Wendell Holmes.

Eugene A. Perry was the originator of the Perry Picture Company established in 1898 with headquarters on Dartmouth Street. The pictures he produced, depicting works of the great masters were widely known and used especially in schools throughout the United States.

Panic of 1893

In 1893, the country was thrown into one of the worst depressions ever experienced. The panic lasted four years. Soup kitchens were set up for the unemployed and charitable groups were required to help in relieving the desperate conditions of the poor. Malden had problems, but met them and survived although progress was hindered and necessary improvements throughout the city were impeded.

Spanish-American War

Nearly one hundred Malden men served in the Army and about fifty in the Navy during the four months following the declaration of war by the United States on April 25, 1898, and until a peace protocol was signed on August 12th, that same year. All men were volunteers.

A finely sculptured military figure stands within a walled park area at Highland Avenue and Pleasant Street, on a portion of what was at one time the Beebe estate. The statue commemorates the Men from Malden who served in this war.

250th Anniversary

From May 20 through May 23, 1899, Malden celebrated its 250th anniversary of incorporation as a town in a style beyond anything ever attempted before or since. The city set aside a large appropriation and the citizens raised another large fund to cover the expenses of the festivities which included: a mammoth parade, a huge banquet, a formal ball, a variety of sports contests, a minstrel show, a program of outstanding musical numbers performed by a large trained chorus of 250 voices, special Sunday services of an historical nature, children's exercises, a mammoth fireworks display, as well as a huge exhibition of priceless items of "historical relics and curios," loaned by a number of individuals for the occasion.

Two events were unusual features of the celebration. A balloon ascension was held at Ferryway Green and witnessed by some ten thousand people, according to the newspaper, and a golf match was scheduled on Converse Links at Pine Banks Park with five ladies and fourteen gentlemen signed up for the contest. This sporting event was acclaimed in an article as:

"The first golf match ever played in this country during the celebration of a town anniversary. It is fair to suppose that in fifty years these four sterling silver cups (won by two ladies and two gentlemen) may be brought out with much satisfaction as momentos of the games at which they were won, now that the game is gaining popularity in this country."

At the banquet which was the concluding event of the observance, each guest received a large, old blue plate as a souvenir, prized now by everyone who has had one handed down in the family. These plates had sketches of early buildings and Maldon and Malden seals etched on them, the design of townsman Ludvig S. Ipsen. Josiah Wedgwood & Sons of Etruria, England, and Richard Briggs Company of Boston manufactured the souvenirs.

Because Malden did not have a building with adequate seating capacity for the indoor programs, a temporary structure officially known as the Anniversary Building was erected on Pleasant Street near Washington Street, a gift of the Honorable Elisha S. Converse. The interior had a seating capacity for thirty-two hundred people on the main floor and gallery, with a stage that could seat an additional three hundred. The building was razed by the end of May to make way for the Auditorium Building which was built later on the same site.

A large companion volume, comparable to the *History of Malden* published by Deloraine P. Corey, Malden's eminent historian, was published in 1900 as a memento of the celebration of the 250th Anniversary. This volume contained all the particulars such as church programs, historic facts, voluminous pictures, displays, speeches, lists of participants and complete descriptions of every indoor and outdoor event.

This celebration was a far more lavish affair than the 200th Anniversary held during one day only, on May 23, 1849 (the first formal observance to honor the founders and also the initial dedication of the Sandy Bank Burying Ground). A procession formed at 10 A.M. on that May morning in front of the Universalist Church on Main Street and marched through Main, Salem, Sprague, Spring,

Main, Mill, Washington, and Pleasant Streets, crossed the railroad to the old Dexter place, continued under the large elms, and countermarched through Pleasant and Main Streets to the Congregational Church at Main Street and Eastern Avenue where it was joined by the ladies who had assembled there. From there the procession continued its march to "Bell Rock Pasture" where the program took place in the open with a completely unobstructed view of the Mystic River. There were seats for 150 persons and others, numbering nearly three thousand, sat on the grass in front of the platform to listen to the oration and the reading of an original poem. Then followed a banquet in an immense pavilion erected close by as "a dining hall" with places provided for nearly two thousand people. Toasts were the highlight of the occasion, all fully recorded in the *Bi-Centennial Book of Malden* for posterity published in 1850. In the evening a brilliant display of fireworks brought the festivities to a close. Many houses were decorated elaborately, some illuminated at night when there were also a band concert and a huge bonfire "blazing from a float upon the fair pond in the centre of the village." (The Dowling building and Jordan Marsh now cover the pond area.)

Development of Banks

Malden is proud of its seven strong banks, all widely known for continued growth and development. The oldest banking institution was started in March, 1833, in the home of Timothy Bailey, at Main and Madison Streets. It had its inception that year when a group of farsighted men banded together and organized the Malden Agricultural & Mechanic Association. At a meeting of citizens held at the hotel of Nathaniel Pratt on November 14, 1850, it was felt necessary to incorporate. In 1851, after a successful beginning, it was chartered by the Commonwealth of Massachusetts as the Malden Bank. At the first directors' meeting, held in Town Hall on July 1, 1851, Timothy Bailey was elected president. After his death in 1853 Mrs. Bailey presented her husband's oil portrait to the bank. Mr. Elisha Converse was elected president in 1865 and served continuously for forty-eight years as director and forty-three years as president. On November 5, 1864, the bank reorganized under the National Bank Act as the First National Bank of Malden. Its first public building was erected in November of 1851 at the corner of Pleasant and Middlesex Streets, where in 1901 its present building was constructed.

On April 2, 1860, Malden Savings Bank was granted a charter.

Officers were elected on May 8th with some of the city's businessmen occupying the positions. They were granted free use of rooms in a portion of the First National Bank headquarters, continuing there for a little over twenty years. In October 1883, with expanded business and the inconvenience caused by two banks carrying on transactions in such limited quarters, arrangements were completed with Mr. H. D. Yerxa to lease quarters in his building on Pleasant Street. In November 1886, the Savings Bank moved to these larger quarters. The bank occupied rooms here for the next sixteen years, then once again it returned to the second floor of the First National Bank building. In April, 1920, the present structure on Main Street, facing Pleasant Street, was built and occupied the following summer. Expansion of these quarters has been necessary several times to meet increased business and provide more modern facilities.

Twenty-seven years later Malden Cooperative Bank was organized by thirty-five Malden citizens. Incorporated on April 27, 1887, it began business the following month. It shared accommodations with the Malden Board of Trade, occupying rooms in the Post Office building on Pleasant Street on the same floor with the Savings Bank (1899). It also moved its headquarters several times: first to the Bailey Building, then to the Board of Trade offices until 1902, next to the second floor of the First National Bank, in 1922 to 353 Main Street, and finally, in 1926, to its own building on Exchange Street. These quarters were remodeled especially for the occasion of its 75th anniversary in 1962.

Malden Trust Company was incorporated by act of the legislature, June 3, 1896. It opened its doors for business December 1, 1896, in the YMCA building on Pleasant Street. Banking facilities proved inadequate for its growing business and in 1915 it occupied its present quarters across the street. It was the first bank in the city to employ a woman and the first to introduce drive-in teller service.

In 1965, the Fellsway Cooperative Bank celebrated fifty years of service, having been established in 1915. It occupied banking quarters on Pleasant Street, at the corner of Linden Avenue, moving later to rooms on Pleasant Street opposite the Malden Electric Company until it occupied its permanent location at 353 Main Street, just south of Malden Square, about 1936.

A group of prominent Malden and Boston businessmen organized another bank in October, 1917, under the name of The Second National Bank of Malden. It continued to prosper under this name until January of 1936 when it was merged with the Middlesex County

The First National Bank on Pleasant Street in 1864 from a woodcut published in Frank Leslie's Illustrated Newspaper.

National Bank which renovated and enlarged the original headquarters at the corner of Main and Ferry Streets.

Various businesses have been located at this prominent corner. In 1800 the highlight of the day in Malden was the coming of the mail by stage coach to the Columbian Tavern. In 1821 the first post office was established on the ground floor. Following its departure to other quarters the tavern became in turn a singing school, billiard hall, meeting hall for a temperance society, and quarters for the district court. In 1916 the famous tavern was one of the three buildings torn down to make room for the Sargeant Building of the Second National Bank followed by the Middlesex County National Bank, there since 1936, having the address of 1 Salem Street, Converse Square.

After occupying temporary quarters for a few weeks, a branch of Century Bank & Trust Company opened large and contemporary facilities at the corner of Ferry Street and Eastern Avenue, on September 8, 1973. It has the most up-to-date banking arrangements featuring three drive-in windows and walk-up conveniences for its customers.

Most of these banks have branches in the community or surrounding shopping areas. These centers have been developing over the last several years and many have been built on the fringes of Malden with ample parking space for the convenience of customers. Broadway, beyond Holy Cross Cemetery, is the site of a new shopping area in Malden but the most recent opened in 1973 off Highland Avenue in the Edgeworth district.

By 1970 Malden was showing signs of a progressive action urban development program on the fringes of Malden Square while apartment houses began springing up in many areas.

District Court

The First District Court of Eastern Middlesex, whose jurisdiction embraces the communities of Malden, Medford, Everett, Melrose, and Wakefield, has been located in Malden since 1874. It moved into its present headquarters on Summer Street at Mountain Avenue in 1922. The court's earliest location was on the second floor of Sargeant's Block at Main and Ferry Streets. It later moved to the Cochrane Block on Ferry Street but the passing trains on the once prosperous Saugus Branch of the Boston & Maine Railroad often interfered with court room decorum. Consequently the court was moved to the Barrett Building in Malden Square and in 1899 to a new court building at 99 Pleasant Street, corner of Linden Avenue.

The Somerset Hotel, which stood on Summer Street opposite the Court House, was destroyed by fire on February 25, 1942, and the site became the parking lot for court officials and the public.

Progressive Era

"The beginning of the period known as The 'Progressive Era' brought many social reforms and industrial advances covering the years from 1900 to 1916. Electric power, gasoline engines, automobiles, aeroplanes, motion pictures, radio and the assembly line, were born during this period, while such social reforms as Labor Unions, the Suffragette movement, new banking and anti-trust laws and laws governing the employment of children, gained momentum."

A smallpox outbreak in 1902 revealed that only seventy-two percent of the populace had been vaccinated. More seriously, the city lacked proper medical facilities to meet epidemic emergencies. Plans were introduced to build a hospital for contagious diseases.

By the turn of the century the city listed nine brick schools and

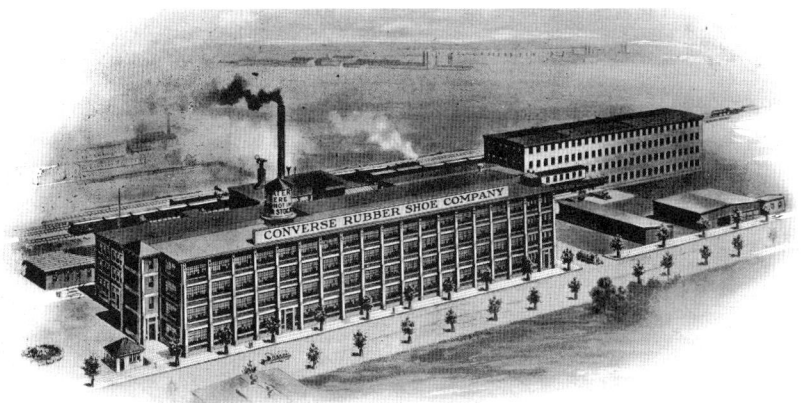

Converse Rubber Shoe Company, one of Malden's biggest industries, was established in January, 1908.

nine wooden ones, with an average attendance of nearly six thousand pupils.

With a growing population the city water supply required enlargement. This was accomplished in 1901 by the addition of two smaller ponds to Spot Pond in addition to a low service reservoir and a high service pumping plant at that site. By 1907 a law was passed providing for the installation of water meters in homes and public buildings. In 1939 additional reservoir enlargement and necessary pipe lines provided for water to be drawn from the Wachusett Reservoir in Clinton.

The Converse Rubber Shoe Company, now the Converse Rubber Corporation, was established in January, 1908, with its factory located on Pearl Street in the Edgeworth district. It was founded by Marquis M. Converse, of Lyme, New Hampshire, who served as president for the first twenty years. The company manufactured rubber boots, shoes, and auto tires and became one of the largest and most important of Malden's industries. It continues its operations in the community although considerably enlarged and modernized. In many instances members of families in Malden and surrounding towns have been on the company payroll for two or three generations. Its "All Star" basketball shoe was one of its "firsts" in athletic footwear and continues to be the choice of many teams.

Growth

Pine Banks Park

In 1881 Elisha S. Converse purchased from Joseph Lynde what was known as the Lynde family farm, consisting of 175 acres. Mr. Converse requested that after his death the land be presented to the communities of Malden and Melrose as a grant to be under the control of the two cities so long as they continued to support it as a public park. Mr. Converse built numerous footpaths and roads winding in all directions and planted handsome shrubs and flower borders to beautify the surroundings.

On December 20, 1904, at a meeting of the Malden Aldermen, Colonel Harry E. Converse, on behalf of himself and sisters offered the 107.5 acres of Pine Banks Park to the cities of Malden and Melrose if they would bear the expense of its upkeep as former Mayor Converse had stipulated. A joint committee from the two cities accepted the offer on January 31, 1905. The Park continues to be operated under a Pine Banks Park Commission, equally represented by both cities and supported and maintained on the same equal basis.

A rustic log cabin, built especially for Mrs. Converse's pleasure by her husband, former Mayor Converse, was long one of the park's attractions. After her death it was used by various groups for meetings and programs until it was destroyed after the 1938 hurricane had damaged it.

The Malden and Melrose Auto Tourist Camp in the park was formally opened for 125 cars on May 9, 1925. It was so badly damaged from falling trees when over five hundred were found uprooted and broken by the 1938 hurricane that the camp area was thereafter abandoned.

Pine Banks Park continues to be a popular place with its well kept flower borders, a small but interesting zoo, and the baseball playing fields and diamond, this latter facility electrically lighted for night games. The park has become a popular spot for bird watchers during spring and fall bird migrations.

Malden's Early "Machines"

With the dawn of the 20th century the automobile became popular. After a trip to France in 1899 Alvin Tufts Fuller, a Malden resident and later a prominent citizen, brought back the first foreign cars, two de Dion Voiturettes which were the first such automobiles to have entered the port of Boston. In his youth Mr. Fuller built up a bicycle

Pine Banks Lodge at the entrance to Pine Banks Park in 1945.

trade in his shop on Cross Street near Tufts Street. Later he became well known when he associated with the automobile business, and headed one of the finest and largest agencies in Boston until his death. The business is carried on by his son, Peter Fuller, at the same location near Cottage Farm Bridge, since renamed Boston University Bridge.

Dr. Thomas J. Springall owned the first automobile in Malden, a one cylinder St. Louis (manufactured by the St. Louis Motor Carriage Company) which made its appearance along the city streets in 1900. By 1905 sixty-six Malden men were listed as automobile owners.

"Big Top" Appearances

In the early 1890's and continuing for a dozen years or more, circus days were an annual event on Pearl Street, about opposite the present Malden High School Stadium. Familiar names, some still remembered, of Barnum & Bailey, Ringling Brothers, Foretaugh, Sells Brothers, created excitement for the town when "the Big Top" was raised for circus performances. "Medicine shows" were earlier attractions, usually held for a week each spring on a vacant lot close by the Pearl Street Fire Station.

Changes in Ward Seven and Ward Two

At the turn of the century the first of the Italian population began to locate in Edgeworth (Ward Two) in increasing numbers. About the same time the nationality picture began to change in Ward Seven. The Chelsea fire on Palm Sunday, April 12, 1908, devastated a large area of that city and created a great influx of Jewish residents to Malden. The first spiritual leader of the Jewish faith had already come to the city and was installed as Rabbi of Beth Israel Synagogue. Rabbi Ber Boruchoff had come first to serve Agudas Achim congregation on Harvard Street and also the Beth Israel congregation when the latter purchased the former Faulkner Methodist Church (then on Faulkner Street) for a synagogue.

A President's Visit

In 1912 the President of the United States, William Howard Taft, visited Malden for "Old Home Week" Parade and a Malden Product Exposition held at the Malden Armory. An official parade held on September 28th was a tremendous occasion. President Taft rode throughout the city over a route along which school children gathered adjacent to their respective schoolhouses, every child proudly waving an American Flag. Each school presented the President with flowers along the way. That same evening more than fifteen hundred persons were present at the banquet held in the armory. It was a gala occasion, long remembered by those who shared in the festivities, for it was the first and only time a President of the United States had visited Malden while in office.

Soldiers' and Sailors' Monument

The Soldiers' and Sailors' Monument is a prominent landmark in Bell Rock Park.

A bronze tablet, first placed on a rock at Bell Rock by the Sons and Daughters of the Revolution, contains the names of all the soldiers and sailors from Malden who served in the War for Independence. It was dedicated with appropriate ceremonies on May 22, 1905.

Three years before, in response to public demand, the city council had purchased the remaining ground to be called "Bell Rock Memorial Park." It was set apart as a permanent memorial to the self sacrifice and patriotism of the founders of the town of Malden and "of the inhabitants thereof in the eras of the Revolution and Civil Wars; dedicated to the promotion of patriotism; to the better understanding of civic rights and duties and to the reception of monuments or memorials for those who have labored for the welfare or defense of the people."

On June 17, 1910, in a downpour of rain, the monument to the Soldiers and Sailors of the Civil War at Bell Rock Memorial Park was unveiled and dedicated. Professor Frederick Law Olmstead's firm designed the park to harmonize with the proposed monument. Two Boston sculptors, Bela L. Pratt and Cyrus E. Dallin, submitted competing designs and the former's work was chosen.

The Revolutionary War Tablet was inserted on the left facade of the terrace entrance wall, inscribed with a complete listing of those who served. A companion tablet on the right facade commemorates the "Founders of Malden whose domestic, social and political life for two generations centered upon this high ground." Recognition of the importance of the parsonage across the street is inscribed on this same tablet. A fifty dollar contribution for the tablets was given by the Malden Chapter of the Sons of the American Revolution, the Malden Historical Society, and the Deliverance Monroe Chapter of the Daughters of the Revolution, with the balance of the expense assumed by the Park Commission. The tablets were unveiled on Columbus Day, October 12, 1910.

The monument entitled "The Flag Defenders" shows an infantryman and a sailor crouching on guard beside the standard bearer, symbolizing the spirit of the great conflict and the youthful and devoted character of the men who made up the two branches of the service. The pedestal was designed by the architect, Clipstone Sturgis; the inscription on the face was the joint effort of Deloraine P. Corey and Sylvester Baxter; the pavement tablet was written by Henry Worcester of the Monument Commission who was a veteran of the Civil War. The cornerstone of the monument was laid on Memorial Day, May 30, 1909, with elaborate Masonic ceremonies conducted by M. W. Dana J. Flanders of Malden, assisted by his Grand Lodge officers and local Masonic organizations. Mr. Corey's inscription to the founders reads:

"In commemoration of the Founders of Malden and of the devotion, sacrifice and Patriotism of those inhabitants thereof who helped in the making and saving of the nation in the days of the struggle for independence and of the period of civil strife."

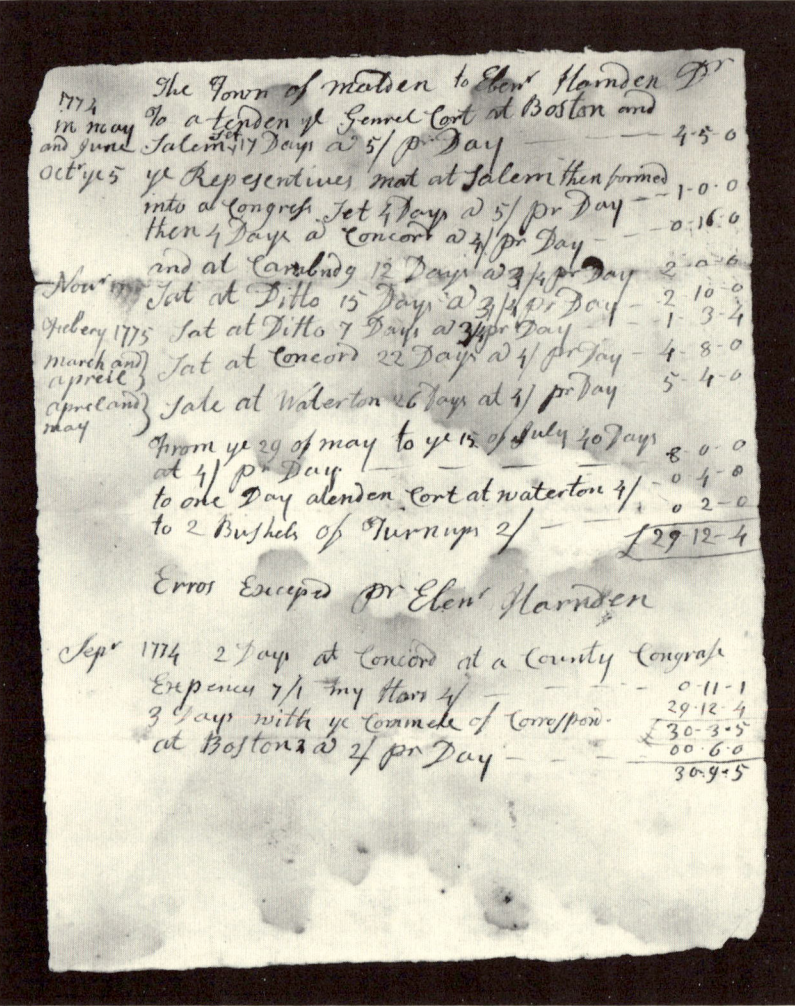

Account of expenses of Captain Ebenezer Harnden in representing the town during 1774. The First Provincial Congress of Massachusetts convened at Salem October 7, 1774, and was dissolved in Cambridge December 10. Malden was represented by Captain Harnden and Captain John Dexter, both former captains of the Malden militia and among the most able and patriotic men of the little town.

New Civic Trends

In the report of the School Committee of September, 1923, it was stated that "the enrollment in the day schools was 8,152; Americanization classes 815; Evening Schools 1170; Continuation classes 205. The so-called Steamer Class prepared foreign-born children with the English language." Periodic examinations were undertaken by school nurses and medical inspectors (doctors) to safeguard against the outbreak of epidemics. Sight & hearing tests were given by the teachers each year, beginning in 1917.

Manual training for boys and home training for girls were valuable courses. Twenty-seven Achievement Clubs, organized in the schools to give instruction in dressmaking, food preparation, poultry, canning and gardening, with a membership of 543, were most successful. A Red Cross Home Nursing Course was conducted for 169 girls in the 8th grades of the school system. A thrift system was initiated in 1922 with eight schools participating. The purpose of this system was to help children form the habit of saving.

The Department of Education for the Commonwealth of Massachusetts named Malden as the city to present a voice demonstration before the State Conference of Music Supervisors on November 16, 1923. This honor was conferred because Malden had developed a High School Musical Club with a chorus of one hundred voices, class singing, and instruction in various instruments.

The schools in 1923 included: Ayers, Cherry Street; Belmont, Cross Street; Browne, Broadway; Center, Ferry Street; Converse, Main & Medford Streets; Daniels, Daniels Street; Emerson, Adams & Highland Avenue; Faulkner, Salem Street; Franklin, Upham Street; Glenwood, Glenwood Street; Greenwood, Faulkner Street; High School, Salem Street; Judson, Walnut Street; Lincoln, Cross Street; Linden, Oliver Street; Maplewood, Salem Street; Pierce, Mountain Avenue; West (later Leonard), Pleasant Street; plus portable schools. The High School had 61 teachers, the other schools 185.

During and following World War I, the Malden War Commission collected historical data and records of all those who served in the war, filing the information for future reference.

Reverting to an earlier custom among the towns and hoping to lift the depressive aftermath of the war, the Mayor recommended a series of band concerts during the summer months to be held in the various parks of the city on specified evenings. These proved to be popular and consequently were continued for the next few summers. The mayor also advocated the erection of a Memorial Building to

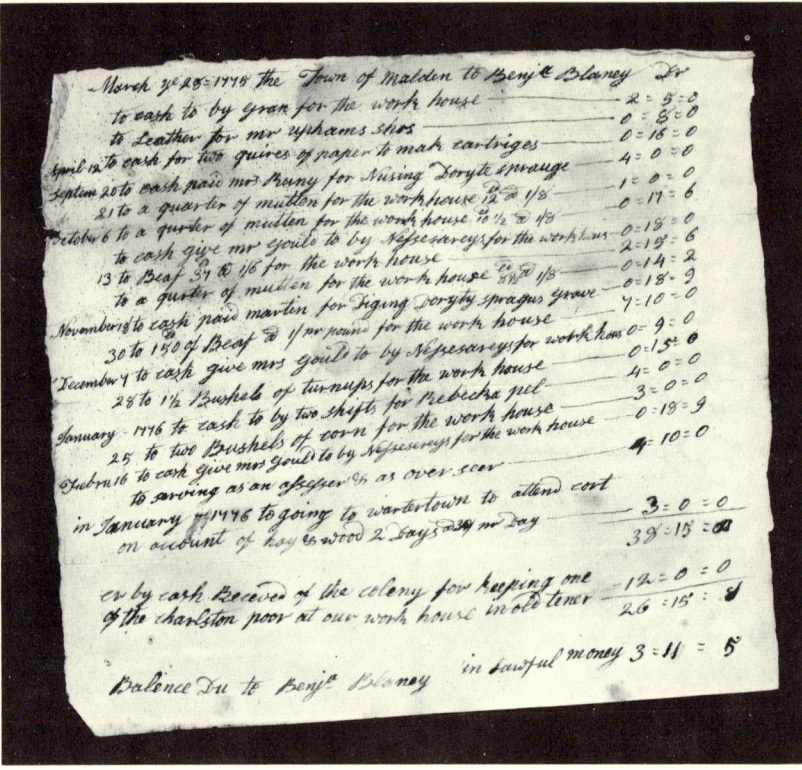

Account of expenses submitted to the town by Captain Benjamin Blaney for supplies in 1775 and '76. Among the entries: "To cash for two quires of paper to make cartriges" on April 12, 1775. Captain Blaney was commander of the Malden troops at the Lexington alarm and while they were stationed at Beacham's Point on the Mystic River until the British evacuated Boston.

honor those who had served in all wars and to provide a convenient auditorium for organizations. Although a committee was appointed and prepared preliminary plans, nothing was accomplished, desperately as Malden needed such a building.

Long after the Cotymore Mill and Dam, the dye-house of the Barretts and the Baldwins, and the rolling mills of the Odiornes and Jonathan Robinson had disappeared, future generations still knew a portion of the land around and adjacent to Spot Pond Brook and the open land there as Cotymore Lea. To commemorate this area an American flag was given to the city by neighbors and Ward Four officials. An impressive ceremony was held in June, 1917, with a flag raising performed by Miss Dorothy D. Kimball, daughter of the Alderman of the Ward, and an exhibition drill by Company L. Eventually, two plaques were inserted in suitable frames and inscribed with the names of men and women who served in World War I and II. Today, a Metropolitan District Commission swimming pool provides pleasure here for the children in summer. It was built on part of the park which was once a pond known as Benson's Ice Pond, where Mr. Benson had ice houses on the easterly bank for storage of cut ice. The plaques have long since disappeared, supposedly were erected on another location, but are still missing.

Children's Recreation Camp

Waite's Mount has been an appropriate location for several projects from the time it first served as a warning signal during the Revolutionary War. Later a standpipe was erected for the city's needs in the 1800's, and subsequently government fortifications were installed. Then the idea of a park was proposed for the area when another project blossomed. The Children's Recreation Camp, on the crest of Waite's Mount was formally dedicated and opened, July 16, 1920, with Mayor John V. Kimball giving the dedication address. As long as the camp operated, a Saturday Carnation Day was held by the city's womens' clubs and other civic groups which sold carnations to provide funds for maintenance of the camp and to provide anemic children outdoor treatment under medical supervision. The camp grew in numbers and about fifty children were cared for during the summers while it was in operation.

Growth

Other 1920 Events

The cornerstone of the Salvation Army building on Irving Street was laid on October first.

Daylight Saving was widely advocated but before signing the Daylight Saving Bill, Governor Calvin Coolidge wired a number of citizens in various parts of the state asking them to telegraph their opinions. Malden's Mayor and a city representative replied that Malden was strongly in favor of the suggested innovation.

"Clean-up Week" in the spring and "Fire Prevention Week" in the fall were carried on city-wide in the 1920's and both were successful.

"Crystal sets" became popular when men, women, and children clamped earphones on their heads to listen to the newest invention, the radio. Later, by turning a single knob, the invention became a fascinating household addition as it received a variety of daily programs and the day's news. Before too long, more elaborate instruments with horn-shaped loudspeakers replaced the earphones.

The Auditorium Building, built by Mr. Converse, was judged one of Malden's finest structures. The street level contained several stores and the post office. It had one of the finest theatres in New England. Many outstanding city events, celebrations, stock company plays, and later movies took place on the huge stage until this section of the building was closed some years after Mr. William Niedner had purchased it.

For well over a quarter of a century, its enormous glittering ballroom was the scene of political and patriotic affairs, Old and New Women's Club meetings (for twenty-five years), Crow Suppers, weddings, and concerts by celebrated artists.

Part 3
The TROUBLED YEARS

During the forty year span between the years 1915 and 1955 the United States agonized through two world wars with their post-war adjustments, the worst depression in her history, and several economic recessions, all interspersed with brief periods of prosperity. At the same time the nation's social fabric deteriorated, first as World War I ushered in a new era of prohibition and permissiveness which was merely an introduction to the "new morality" which emerged after World War II. These were troubled years for all Americans but their time-honored Puritan heritage enabled many in Malden to face difficulties and temptations calmly and with courage.

AS MALDEN ENTERED WORLD WAR I in 1917, it showed more changes. Homes were equipped with oil stoves for cooking, and kerosene water heaters and wooden ice boxes were welcomed as a modern means of housekeeping. Fortunate were the families who could enjoy floor registers in first floor rooms with heat provided by a coal-burning furnace. Wheezing gaslight jets were another welcome improvement as the jets shed dim lighting from high ceiling fixtures. The Malden and Melrose Gas Light Company first furnished gas, mainly for lighting, to Malden residents in 1860. In 1886 the Malden Electric Company installed electric street lighting. Horse-drawn wagons began to be replaced with motorized vehicles.

"As the European War progressed, Malden men once again left their peaceful occupations to serve their country. On August 25, 1917, Company L 5th Infantry, Massachusetts National Guard with 3 officers and 150 enlisted men were called into the federal service. A mammoth farewell celebration was held for the entire company on Ferryway Green." While this unit was in service a company of the State Guard was organized at the armory and designated Company L 101st Infantry Massachusetts National Guard. One figure gives 3,000 Malden citizens as serving in World War I, but as few as 2,900 to as many as 4,200 soldiers were listed "from Malden" since recognition was given to those born, raised, and living in Malden before or after serving. Approximately a hundred men from Malden received decorations for gallantry in action, sixty-nine were killed in action or died from other causes while in the service.

A Malden man became the country's first prisoner of war. As Chief Gunner's Mate in the U.S. Navy, Joseph L. Delaney was captured and held prisoner on a German submarine. Malden also provided all five of the first Massachusetts men to be certified for duty. William Austin Trafton, of Malden's Company L, National Guard, was the first Malden boy to make the supreme sacrifice in World War I.

At home, Victory Gardens, War Bond Drives and work in munitions and other war related industries occupied the time of every citizen able to contribute. Children who were helping out on the farms were reluctant to return to school at summer's end. The school board made a special appeal to parents to see that all pupils returned to their classes.

That first Christmas of the war, Company L received a letter twenty feet long signed by the mayor and the townspeople. Knitting articles for the men in the service became a steady occupation for many women. Shortages in numerous food items were accepted

Soldiers and Sailors monument in Bell Rock Park.

cheerfully by those left at home but limited coal supplies added burdens to home and business heating conveniences.

"In the fall of 1918, the city suffered a Spanish influenza outbreak. As the epidemic spread and the toll of sick and dying rose, the State Guard erected tents on the lawn of the Contagious Hospital on Forest Street to alleviate the overcrowded conditions at Malden Hospital. As the outbreak worsened the city took on a somber appearance. The Mayor ordered all public buildings closed. The churches were shut in late September and for the month of October. The Telephone Company was requested to fumigate its pay booths and public telephones. Before the year ended the worst was over and the city struggled back to normalcy but not without many families losing someone within their immediate circle."

World War I ended with the Armistice being declared on November 11, 1919, and all of Malden, like other cities, celebrated the event, believing this conflict had ended war for all time.

Dedication of plaque in Bell Rock Park commemorating the founders of Malden and the legend of The Parsonage in October, 1910.

Aftermath of World War I

The city more or less stood still during the years of World War I with few improvements undertaken although many were needed. By January 1, 1920, Malden had the highest tax rate of any municipality in the state, its borrowing capacity being the lowest in its history. With rigid economy and by combining several city departments, the situation was eased somewhat and within the next two years the efficiency of the city's administration had improved. One forward step to help increase revenues was the revision of building laws in anticipation of apartment construction. Ways of inducing new industries, especially manufacturers, were studied as a means of increasing the city's prosperity.

With the ending of the war a critical unemployment situation developed during 1920-1921. This problem was eased with the employment of 682 citizens, mostly ex-servicemen, on city projects. Paving of streets was begun and continued over the next few years as finances permitted, using the unemployed. This project helped improve the poor travel conditions throughout the city, since dirt roads required regular summer watering to cut down the dust. Several such projects benefited the city and helped relieve unemployment.

By 1921 Malden stood near the top in the state when Americanization Classes were started by the School Department, the financial burden being equally divided between the state and city. Twenty-two classes with an approximate attendance of five hundred persons helped alleviate the difficult language problem with an ever-increasing number of aliens settling in the city.

Following a spirited parade from City Hall, sponsored by the Malden Rotary Club, a grand official opening of Malden's High School Athletic Field was held on October 28th. A flag raising opened the first football game in the new stadium on Pearl Street, near Chester Street, with a 12-0 win over Cambridge Latin. Dedication took place the following summer after the landscaping was completed. This new field was a far cry from the former one on Bryant Street where football games were held for some years. It was later known as Macdonald Stadium in memory of a former coach.

A Commercial School was well established, a Hebrew Free School had recently opened, and the Malden School of Religious Education was spreading its fame among the surrounding communities. The public school population of 7,808 required 230 teachers. The three Parochial schools flourished with three thousand students in attendance. By the end of 1921 prosperity was returning to Malden. Thirty-one churches cared for the spiritual needs of the community. There were sixty-five fraternal societies, all well established, and thirty-nine other organizations of a charitable nature and some of a social nature. Three well equipped theatres and a fourth in process of construction offered a broad range of entertainment. The Orpheum featured the antics of Charlie Chaplin and Mary Pickford, the Auditorium had both a stock company and movies with weekly serials of "The Perils of Pauline" to keep the audiences in suspense, and the Mystic and the Strand presented vaudeville at first and later movies. The Strand opened at the time when the Charleston competition was in vogue and prizes encouraged many young people to compete. The opening of the Granada came later, but by 1973 it was the only theatre left in the city showing motion pictures.

The veterans of each of the various wars had their own organizations. Post 40 G.A.R. with its auxiliary bodies served the men of the Civil War. Moses B. Lakeman Encampment of the United Spanish War

Veterans and its affiliated bodies still boasted an active membership. Post 69, American Legion of the World War I, and Post 639 Veterans of Foreign Wars, together with their various auxiliaries attracted the younger veterans.

Many aspects of daily living changed considerably during the new decade and few in the nation, or the city of Malden for that matter, realized that life would never be quite the same again. Elaborate balls, huge fancy banquets, receptions of glittering fashions, and large parades were commonplace during the 1920's and continued until World War II. An evening of fun had always crowned the annual Crow supper of the Deliberative Assembly when a large attendance assembled after the annual election.

Malden had a lamplighter to light the gas lamps along the Fellsway until the gas fixtures were replaced by electric street lights. Thomas E. Sheedy, a Malden native who lived his entire life in the city, fulfilled this duty and he was a familiar sight as he "made the nights a little brighter" during these years.

On January 30, 1921, the Harriet E. Sawyer Home for Aged Women, formerly the Millett Mansion at 22 Parker Street, was opened with services of dedication. The home was named for Mrs. Sawyer, its founder and a state vice president of the W.C.T.U. The project had begun three years previously as the White Ribbon Home for aged members of the Massachusetts W.C.T.U. in buildings at Camp Devens in Ayer in 1917. These facilities had been used as a hostelry for women relatives of the soldiers then stationed at the camp.

In 1920 the League of Women Voters had been founded as a prelude to women's suffrage which became an accomplished fact by 1921 when the required number of states ratified the 19th Amendment. In 1924 two women in Malden were elected to the city council for the first time.

Malden launched its Symphony Orchestra at Malden High School with a fine program on May 3, 1921. It became a worthy contemporary of the famed Schubert and Malden Musical Clubs and the Weltman Conservatory School of Music.

Many improvements were undertaken from 1921 to 1924: a Field House was built at Cradock Park to relieve a troublesome condition there. Six parks in the city provided skating in winter and various sports the rest of the year. Competitive games arranged by the Park Department drew crowds of young people when these were publicized for special occasions.

Ward rallies were popular during the years candidates were

Principal Richard W. Nutter and pupils of the Center School taking magazines for soldiers to the Malden Public Library in April, 1917.

campaigning throughout the city, especially the night before election when tensions were tight and enthusiasm high. Schools were crowded in some sections and ideas for improving them were being suggested by officials and parents alike. The superintendent of schools recommended establishment of junior high schools to relieve overcrowded conditions.

Both the sewer and water systems were extended and additional hydrants were installed wherever there were new businesses and housing. Among these buildings was the Dowling structure at the corner of Pleasant and Main Streets. This fine addition to the city improved the appearance of the Malden Square area. Exchange Street was extended from Middlesex to Main Street, widened and paved, making this a traffic throughway parallel to Pleasant Street, and these two streets were eventually made one-way. With the increase of automobiles a traffic squad was established in 1923. This same year all school buildings in the city (seventeen in number) were equipped with new fire alarm boxes.

When Malden entered upon its fortieth year of municipal life (1922), the population had grown from 12,779 when the city charter was granted to 49,103.

World War I Victory parade in Malden, May 30, 1919. Photo by Herbert A. Hall.

In 1923, the Yale Knitting Company, established in 1910, enlarged its plant. The next year the *Malden Evening News* moved from the old Clifford-Black Building on Main Street to its present new headquarters at Ferry and Prescott Streets.

In 1926 S. S. Kresge Company built two stores on Pleasant Street. That same year Perry Pictures moved from upper Middlesex Street to a newly constructed building on Mountain Avenue, opposite Malden Armory. This building, costing $100,000, was later occupied and owned by the Lawson Machine Tool Company until the plant moved from Malden. The building was torn down eventually to make room for an apartment house which opened in 1972.

A post office was built on Ferry Street on the opposite corner from the Malden News Building. The Granada Theatre was erected on Pleasant Street adjacent to Malden Square, opening its doors on November 13, 1926, with a seating capacity for twenty-five hundred persons.

A day nursery was erected on Ferry Street opposite the Malden News Building, and this filled a great need for working mothers. Here they could leave their children under trained supervision. The Community Nursing Association has been of great benefit to the citizens of the city from its inception. The Ida M. Converse Building next to the Day Nursery has housed several agencies connected with Family Service in Malden.

Gradually many of the city's older wooden buildings were torn down and replaced by more modern structures. Two new businesses were welcomed: an immense grocery store opened by J. B. Blood & Company on Main Street south of the Square, and a large A & P on Pleasant Street. A new office building was occupied by the Gas & Electric Company while William T. Grant, a Malden native, opened one of his 5c to $1.00 department stores at 80 Pleasant Street.

275th Anniversary

Malden's 275th Anniversary was celebrated on May 25, 1924, with an impressive evening program held in the Auditorium Theatre. Rev. Isaac Lothian Seymour, Vicar of All Saints in Maldon, England, was a special guest of the city. Although it was but a one evening occasion, the Order of Exercises, arranged by the presiding officer, the Honorable Alfred E. Cox, proved an outstanding program. It included musical numbers by the Schubert Club, Edward L. MacArthur, director; invocation by the Rev. Richard Neagle; addresses by the Mayor, Governor Channing H. Cox, Rev. Seymour, Lieutenant Governor Alvan T. Fuller, Honorable Arthur H. Wellman, Councilman Fletcher Sprague Hyde, and Honorable Harvey L. Boutwell. A concluding speech was delivered by Honorable George Howard Fall.

A blue hardcover book describing the entire proceedings was published and distributed by the Malden Historical Society in 1925. On the final page of this well arranged publication one of Malden's most illustrious men received a well deserved tribute. Honorable Alfred E. Cox, who had been chairman of the 275th Anniversary Exercises had died, May 22, 1925, just as the book was going to press. Mr. Cox occupied a unique place in Malden's history. Here follows a portion of the tribute to Mr. Cox.

"Born 31 August, 1848, while yet a mere stripling, he showed himself to be a political genius. Politics, outside of his business, was the pursuit of his life. He studied it days and dreamed over it nights. He played it as he would a game of chess and office-holders were the pawns of the game which he moved according to his will. The late Senator, Henry Cabot Lodge, once declared that Mr. Cox was 'the ablest and most astute politician he had ever known, in city, state or national politics.'

"But it was in Malden that his political capacity found its fullest expression. Here he ruled local affairs with a rod of iron. He made and unmade selectmen, councilmen, aldermen, mayors, according to the necessities of the situation, as he viewed it, and never was there a hint of graft or corruption. All went to him for instructions and received instructions from him . . . His advice was sought and followed as long as his life lasted . . . Malden evolved one star of the first political magnitude."

Worst Depression in History

Within a few years the country plunged into the worst depression in its history. The Stock Market crashed on Black Thursday, October 24, 1929. By the end of 1930 the effects of the tragic depression were felt in Malden. Nevertheless the city managed to provide for its needy citizens at less expense per capita than did any other municipality. Many people held on to their savings as long as possible. March 4, 1933, when the banks closed, was designated by the President of the United States as "a bank holiday." Many residents of Malden, like countless others throughout the country, lost real estate investments and much of their savings during these years.

Between 1933 and 1935 one recovery program after another was begun by authorities in Washington, starting with the Civilian Conservation Corps, (CCC) for the unemployed youth. A Works Progress Administration (WPA) was established with three large arts projects. Malden benefited by sharing in several of the emergency projects. By 1933 Malden's Welfare and Relief Departments were distributing relief orders for its most desperately needy citizens. These orders were honored by local merchants at personal sacrifice in many instances.

Malden's Unemployment Committee, in conjunction with the Chamber of Commerce, raised funds to employ men at $4.00 per day to work at Forest Dale Cemetery and Pine Banks Park, as well as in other locations where repairs were needed. The other cemeteries were improved when surrounding walls were built by the unemployed. A $25,000 appropriation was authorized in 1933 by the city for public works and employed men for filling and grading public parks throughout the city. Another $54,000 allotment improved streets and sidewalks and paid for construction of sewer and surface drainage. Malden, like other cities, shared in WPA projects which provided financial aid to those hardest hit by the Depression. The federal aid

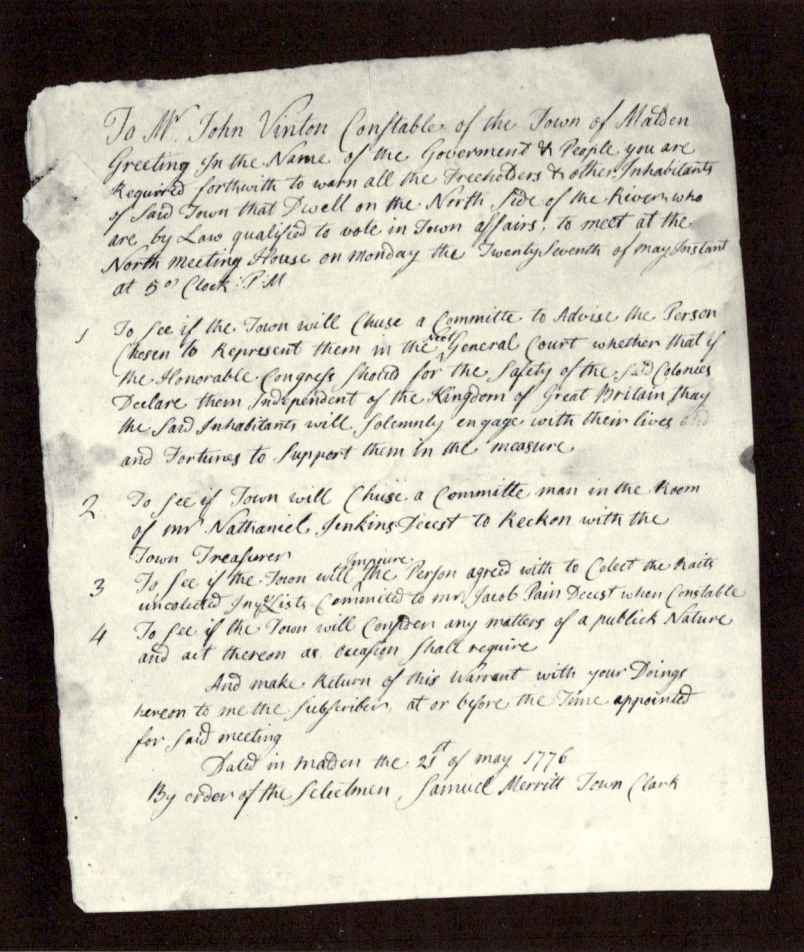

Warrant for the Town Meeting, dated May 21, 1776, in response to the resolution of the Massachusetts House of Representatives calling upon the towns to . . . "instruct their representatives upon this great question" (of independence). The men of Malden responded before their fellows of other towns . . . the instructions of Malden preceding those of Boston by three days.

continued until early in 1940 when applications for assistance showed a satisfactory decline.

A coal shortage caused suffering in the city and many organizations were generous in contributing to the Mayor's Coal Fund. This provided financial assistance at a time when so many people were out of work and/or unable to pay for fuel. Churches united in union services for over two months to help conserve fuel.

In 1935, Malden became the first community in the state to be thoroughly covered by a controlled survey. This action proved invaluable in constructive town planning for sewer and highway construction, irrigation and flood control, power and pipe line extensions.

Hurricane Disasters

On September 18, 1836, the worst tropical storm in forty years roared into New England tearing down trees and electrical wires and causing great damage to homes and public buildings with loss of heat and light for several days. This storm was outdone by the hurricane that struck Malden and all surrounding communities on September 21, 1938, when the city suffered the worst hurricane ever recorded in this region. For the first time in Malden's history the Militia was ordered to patrol the city to protect property of its citizens. The damage reached gigantic proportions and caused great anxiety and serious problems. Telephone and signal systems were out of order when wires were brought down. Electricity was shut off and some areas of the city were without light, heat, and power for days and in some areas for as much as two weeks, exceeding the inconvenience of the earlier storm. The damage was discouraging and expensive. Hundreds of shade trees were uprooted and others were seriously hurt. Many a church steeple fell during the violent storm but fortunately Malden's churches escaped serious trouble. It took considerable time to clear up the debris and repair the damage, but certain parks and highways, once beautifully landscaped by handsome shade trees, could not have their beauty restored.

Other Changes

The year 1938 saw the end of the trolley cars and the introduction of a trackless trolley system which operated about twenty-five years before giving way to buses.

By this time, air service was popular and automobiles had become a necessity for many.

In 1932 with the arrival of Brother Gilbert, C.F.X., sports at the Catholic High School Stadium took on new dimensions. "During his lifetime his name became a legend in baseball circles. As the discoverer of Babe Ruth his fame spread as his protege became world renowned." Brother Gilbert died in 1947. One year later the stadium was rededicated to his memory and thereafter became known as the Brother Gilbert Memorial Stadium. This is a busy and exciting place when games are played here beside Medford Street, between Commercial Street and the old canal.

World War II

Pearl Harbor was attacked on December 7, 1941, and the world was plunged into another global conflict. Once again Malden citizens came to their country's defense. More than six thousand men and women served in the various branches of the armed forces and over 230 lost their lives while in service. An army of defense workers volunteered for work in war plants and served at air raid centers. Volunteers sold War Bonds and collected necessary war items like foil. Rationing became a way of life with stamps being required for the purchase of certain foods.

Blackouts were ordered for a time when even street lighting was prohibited. On March 6, 1942, the entire city was plunged into darkness as a complete blackout test was held in anticipation of a real air raid. Only those persons necessary to public service were permitted in the streets after dark. If lights were to be used, every house and public building was required to use blackout shades or curtains. Air raid shelters were established about the city, well manned and effectively serviced. At the end of the shelter requirement, awards were given to all those who had served a certain number of hours or had performed Red Cross work. Some 1,856 defense workers guarded the city on March 6th during the first blackout air raid test. All workers were at their posts within 20 minutes from the time the sirens started blowing at 9:30 P.M. Malden was the first city to inaugurate such a test. With only two slight incidents, the test was duly declared a complete success. People had become accustomed to using the blackout curtains each night and cooperation was a patriotic duty required of everyone.

Many Malden citizens and organizations, as well as business

firms, gave unstintingly of their time, energy, and financial resources to the war effort. School children bought bonds at the schools and this patriotic participation was highly praised and encouraged by the school personnel.

Malden Girl Scouts gave a mobile kitchen to the Canteen Corps for civil defense work and the Middlesex Amusement Company presented a Ford ambulance for civil defense needs. Among the women's clubs, Old and New organized a Red Cross Motor Corps with fifteen members. Malden High School held war production training classes using machines provided by the Lawson Machine Tool Company. The staff of the Malden Public Library collected nearly 3,000 volumes for the armed forces. Every woman who was able, kept busy knitting for service men, selling bonds, collecting foil, rolling bandages, helping at Service Canteen Centers on Boston Common, and serving in other ways.

Ten thousand persons jammed Malden Square one day in 1942 and twenty thousand War Bonds were sold during the greatest sale of the year.

Over two thousand ballots were mailed to those serving in the armed forces who had retained interest in hometown elections. Over fifteen hundred ballots were returned to the City Clerk's office whose staff worked overtime to provide this privilege for those away from home. These items are but a few of the numerous contributions made by the people of Malden during these war years.

The second World War required extra police precautions and an appeal to civic-minded citizens produced a heart-warming response. In Malden 267 people volunteered and an auxiliary police force was organized. Later, the establishment of training programs enabled these officers to keep up with new developments in police work.

In December of 1942, President Franklin D. Roosevelt's request was finalized with the issuing of ration books. "The average motorist was given two or three gallons a week; needy or privileged persons received more." The rationing was very effective, cutting automobile mileage in half the first year despite black market problems. Rationing was instituted primarily to save tires and gasoline.

Victory Ship For Malden

In the summer of 1944 the city was honored when a Victory ship, S.S. *Malden Victory* was launched. The keel was laid in Baltimore and sixty-six days later the ship was built and ready for service. It was one of the first of ninety-eight ships, built and named for two cities from every state in the Union. The *S.S. Malden Victory* had a gross tonnage of 7,612 tons, was 455 feet long, and had a speed of 15.5 knots.

She was christened by Mrs. Daniel F. McBride, mother of seven sons who were serving in the armed forces. Five local war industries, Lawson Machine Tool Company, National Company, Converse Rubber Shoe Company, Charles Niedner's Company, and Robertson Company, contributed to a gift fund. An abbreviated "History of Malden," a 200 volume library and plaques mounted with the City Seal, were presented to the ship's officers and men together with personal gifts.

Malden's Victory ship served throughout the war. She was released for cargo service then reclaimed during the Korean conflict. She was last seen in Yokohama Harbor in 1952 heavily laden and earning her second service stripes. When recalled to duty in 1965 she was not able to complete her first trip carrying supplies to Vietnam because of neglect during the intervening years.

V-E Day was wildly celebrated by the Allies but for Americans an even bigger celebration came on August 14, 1945, remembered as V-J Day which noted the end of the war with Japan.

Two tablets listing those who served in World War I and World War II were inserted in sections in the Memorial Arch at the southeast corner at Bell Rock Park. Both, defaced by vandals, were removed sometime ago. Plaques were presented to the city by various wards and groups to be erected in specific spots in the community. Some are still in place, several have been destroyed.

War's Aftermath

The war ended in 1945 with the surrender of Japan. As veterans returned home the city began the difficult task of recovery. In 1947 Malden faced the largest increase in its annual budget ever experienced. Reconversion to peacetime economy would prove a severe task. Maintenance of schools and public buildings had been neglected, most public utilities and equipment had deteriorated. The housing situation was critical with war veterans returning home and overcrowding conditions created health and sanitary hazards. The Great Depression had undermined the city's progress and its financial ability to improve such conditions. Neglect and shabbiness were far too common.

In 1949 Malden faced another fuel crisis. A committee was estab-

S.S. Malden Victory was launched at Bethlehem-Fairfields shipyard at Baltimore, Maryland on October 22, 1944.

lished to alleviate the problem and to provide, as far as possible, oil or kerosene for those unable to obtain fuel through their usual sources.

"That same year of 1949 there was a severe epidemic crisis with 35 cases of polio, the first recurrence since 1916. Clinics and inoculation centers were set up to protect the citizens until a vaccine was proven safe and accepted by the populace."

There were forty-two physicians with offices in Malden who were ready to help.

Tercentenary Observance

Amid its many problems and perplexities the city observed its Tercentenary from June 12 to 17, 1949, with a huge parade and an elaborate pageant titled, "Cavalcade of the Centuries," covering three hundred years in Malden in 20 episodes with a cast of twelve hundred men and women. It was produced at the Pearl Street Stadium during the celebration week. The pageant demonstrated, by means of stage scenes, Malden's history from the time of the Indians who had roamed the region, down through the years to 1949. The parade was

Converse Square in July, 1948. Photo by William P. Morgan.

held on Sunday, June 12th, and daily events were provided for the younger generation. The Mayor of Maldon, England, with other public dignitaries were guests of the city and of Mayor Fred I. Lamson.

A Tercentenary Booklet (paper back) with gold covers and blue printing (the colors of Malden High School) was published by the city at the time of Malden's celebration. Earlier in the season, during the week of May 8 to 15, First Church, Congregational, celebrated its 300th

Anniversary in conjunction with the First Parish, Universalist. A week-long program of services, dinners, young people's events, luncheons, teas and pageants was held by both churches to commemorate the founding and growth of the ancient church which resulted in the town's establishment.

Television Appears

The first public TV broadcast in the United States took place in 1930. Televising on a regular service basis began in this country on April 30, 1939, in connection with the opening of the New York World's Fair.

As television became a part of the normal living routine in more and more families, moving-picture and legitimate theaters suffered a severe decline in patronage. Thousands of theaters closed and stage productions drew fewer crowds. It was not until the early 1970's that many smaller cinemas were built near or within shopping centers. The novelty of TV had worn off with the production and showing of poorer programs.

Korean Conflict

The Korean conflict (never an officially declared war) began June 25, 1950, with the invasion of South Korea by the armies of the North Korean Communists. It lasted three years until an armistice was signed July 27, 1953. It did not impose any unusual restrictions nor did it demand any real sacrifice in Malden. Malden was represented by five men who served in the Marine Corps, eight in the Army, one in the Air Force and three in the Navy.

Hurricane Edna

On September 11, 1956, Hurricane Edna created severe damage although its effects were far less devastating than the hurricane of 1938. Flooding was severe, many trees were uprooted and many business plants and homes were damaged.

Part 4
REBIRTH

The dominant achievement of the past two decades has been the rebirth of Malden's inner city. The downtown business area of Malden, like those of many older American cities, had gradually deteriorated as buildings outlived their usefulness, urban decay set in, and people began to desert established businesses for the newer outlying shopping centers. Acknowledging this condition and vowing to correct it, Malden's leaders set out to rebuild the heart of their metropolis. Undoubtedly this was the city's most significant and costly undertaking. Furthermore, it was a fitting accomplishment to culminate Malden's more than three centuries of history.

A GROUP OF INTERESTED CITIZENS with urban renewal in mind pioneered a change of government in 1952, with a "Plan D for Malden" committee. In 1881 with its rapid population growth Malden had adopted a city government with a mayor and bicameral legislative branches. By 1952 this form of administration had become cumbersome and out-of-date. To improve the efficiency of the city's top administration, a mayor and an eleven man council was recommended to the people. In 1955 the change was accepted by an overwhelming vote. The new government was inaugurated January 1, 1958, with the original charter still in use but educational matters were now the concern of a five member school committee.

With the inauguration of Mayor Walter J. Kelliher a year of ambitious planning to rebuild Malden to a greater potential was undertaken. A law passed nine years earlier was activated to set in motion an extensive urban renewal program.

In 1957 Malden faced a difficult problem. A severe transition in Malden's population had taken place during the previous decade. A city of more than sixty thousand had become a victim of urban blight. Families, following the trend of the times, began moving out into smaller towns where space for community growth was attractive, especially among young homemakers. Churches in the city suffered from this change. Business and industry were leaving, neighborhoods were rapidly deteriorating, schools and many public buildings had become obsolete or inadequate. The Depression had undermined the city's progress and made it financially impossible to improve the unfortunate conditions so prevalent during the decades following.

Malden's recovery from the aftermath of World War II and its effects began in 1958 with the establishment of the Malden Redevelopment Authority and its obligation to institute a federally aided urban renewal program. Malden was foremost among surrounding communities, comparable in size, to meet the distressing conditions.

By 1961 certain sections of the city had well organized plans. Malden was one of the first municipalities in the Commonwealth to determine the feasibility of accepting federal aid. That same year nearly $3 million worth of new construction had been completed. New schools, housing, and public utilities paved the way for Malden's rebirth. In less than fifteen years Malden had recovered from the devastating aftermath of World War II.

Malden was the first Massachusetts city to establish a Code Department with inspections to ensure that all buildings, public as well as private, met certain health and safety standards. This was

Veterans' housing at Tartikoff Park in July, 1948. Photo by William P. Morgan.

accomplished during 1962. Thereafter urban renewal, anti-poverty programs, and an educational program were made possible through liberal aid from the state and federal governments.

Work started in the Suffolk-Faulkner area in December, 1962. Demolition was begun and continued steadily but further progress toward redevelopment did not materialize. "Weeds, not deeds" became a campaign issue in the fall of 1963. Then gradually the area spurted with new homes, moderate income units, and new businesses. The Eastern Shopping Plaza, erected and owned by Frank Chick, became "The First Commercial Center in the city to be constructed on reclaimed land involved in an urban renewal project." A Catholic High School was built, a synagogue opened. With the new housing project for veterans in Linden, a new Linden School was erected to accommodate the children living in this development.

The Suffolk-Faulkner neighborhood redevelopment covered 208 acres and received $12 million urban renewal funding. A total of 226 units of moderate income housing became known as the Bowdoin Apartments and opened in December, 1964. Two other housing projects developed in the same area. One contained one hundred units for the elderly on the south side of the former Suffolk Square and just across Willow Street on the north side. The other was a corporation formed by members of Congregation Agudas Achim which sponsored 108 units of moderate income housing similar to the Bowdoin complex. A business block was developed on Eastern Avenue in the same locality and private homes also rose as attractive landscaping added to the improvement program.

The next area of redevelopment was the Charles Street project, covering twenty-three acres, in which demolition began on March 15, 1965. This was a unique procedure. Profiting from unfortunate circumstances in the Suffolk-Faulkner redevelopment, when land laid idle for some length of time after buildings had been demolished, this second area was entirely committed before work began with specific firms and businesses signed up for definite land areas. This was one of the city's oldest and most neglected districts. With industrial development and a neighborhood area improvement program, the necessary and warranted growth of Malden was ensured. In 1967 Malden was selected as an "All American City" by *Look Magazine*. By the beginning of the 1970's the city ranked 18th in size in the Commonwealth and 2nd in urban renewal.

In 1963 Malden became one of the first cities in the state to explore the possibilities of federal assistance for her schools. With funds provided by the National Defense Education Act, a language laboratory was installed in the Lincoln Junior High School. Similar facilities were authorized for the Beebe and Browne Junior High Schools. Equipment and materials to improve the teaching of science, mathematics, and foreign languages were also purchased. Funds were obtained to improve the facilities of the Guidance Department, and for the first time in its history, Malden High School became a testing center for the College Entrance Examination Board.

In 1969 the population stood at 58,213, with 27,266 enrolled voters. Board of Health clinics provided vaccines for the prevention of childhood diseases, freeing the city from the dreaded epidemics which had afflicted so many children and adults in previous years.

More than 250 elderly Malden residents were provided hot meals at noontime on school days through participation in a program operated jointly by the state and city agencies. Malden was one of the few Massachusetts communities which offered this program.

McFadden Memorial Manor in the Forestdale area has provided for the city's "extended care" patients at this medical center.

In 1967, there were 261 social, civic and fraternal organizations actively functioning within the city. A Malden Council for the Ageing was established in the spring of 1960. A center opened on Washington Street South and moved, a short time later, around the corner on

Exchange Street. Programs of varying kinds are provided and well attended.

The Chamber of Commerce provided the following facts for the middle 1960's:

"Over 6,000 people were employed in the city in its more than 200 diversified industrial firms, which produced among a variety of items: rubber boots, shoes, soap, toilet goods, paints and brushes, airplane parts, shoe polish, radios, machine tools, knitted wear, boxes, plastics and atomic clocks. Its estimated 600 business firms, both wholesale and retail, employed more than 8,000 wage earners. It had become known world-wide for its rubber boots, sneakers and shoes. Malden, by this time, served 300,000 people within a trading area, covering a radius of 100 square miles. It continued to be a religious center with at least 34 churches or religious societies.

"In the same period, there were special classes supervised by the public school department for the blind, mentally retarded, physically handicapped, and mentally gifted, with adult civic education, evening school and kindergarten. Six parochial schools had an enrollment of 1,000 pupils."

Jet Travel

In 1922 the General Court authorized that an aircraft landing field be laid out at East Boston. Thereafter, in due time, land was filled and construction of landing strips developed into a small airport. With the expansion of airlines, terminal facilities and landing areas, Logan International Airport rates as one of the country's most modern airports.

In 1959, jet airplanes were inaugurating passenger service to the west coast and abroad. Malden grew well aware of air travel with an airport so close at hand. Logan Airport was built on filled-in land bordering Boston Harbor in East Boston.

Progress in the 1970's

Malden's population in 1970 numbered 56,127 with 28,181 registered voters. During this same year 299 new dwelling units were constructed. The mayor-city council type of government continued to run the city. Although Malden remained primarily as a residential community, during the 1970's its growing business development was contributed in good measure by the urban renewal progress. There were 1,077 firms doing business, employing an average of

14,548 persons with an annual payroll of $101,441,814. Figures in October of 1973 showed a population count of 56,282.

The city became a member of the Northeast Metropolitan Regional Vocational School District located on the Breakheart Reservation in the Wakefield and Saugus area. There had been a Vocational High School within the Malden school system for some years. On October 1, 1970, the count showed there were 10,420 pupils attending public schools and 411 teachers were employed within the system. In addition 1,676 pupils were enrolled in private schools.

Seventy acres of land had been set aside for parks and playgrounds with an annual appropriation of well over $20,000 allocated for a varied program of activities for children and sponsored by the Recreation Commission. Supervised recreational programs in the city's thirteen parks attract nearly forty thousand children a year. Winter programs continued in various activities indoors and numerous outings were planned for summer trips. Cradock Park on the Fellsway in Ward 2 was renamed the John M. Devir Park in recognition of the father of a former mayor who lived in that Ward. He was for many years a leading political figure in both the town and the city government. Three other smaller parks are in need of improvement and beautification.

The Malden Housing Authority provided housing units for the elderly through the "Turnkey Housing" program. Modern facilities continued to be built in various sections of the city with well over fifteen hundred units opened by 1973. Plans for more such housing are still in the formative stage.

The Malden Public Library with its four branches provides not only books but also phonograph records, newspapers (back issues of some are on microfilm), motion picture films, and filmstrips. Books are provided for shut-ins by library messengers. Pre-school story hours attract children in this age group. The Good Reading and Discussion Group, holding sixteen sessions a year, completed its twenty-sixth year in 1973. A certain number of free lectures, set up under the Robinson Fund, are arranged by the library trustees each year during the winter season. This continues to be a most popular series.

The 1970 census shows a population of sixty thousand residing within an area of 4.8 square miles which is less than a third of the Malden (and originally, Mystic Side) territory of 1640.

Six bus lines had been franchised by the state to serve the city. Over 100 established trucking lines have provided competitive service, locally, and to distant points.

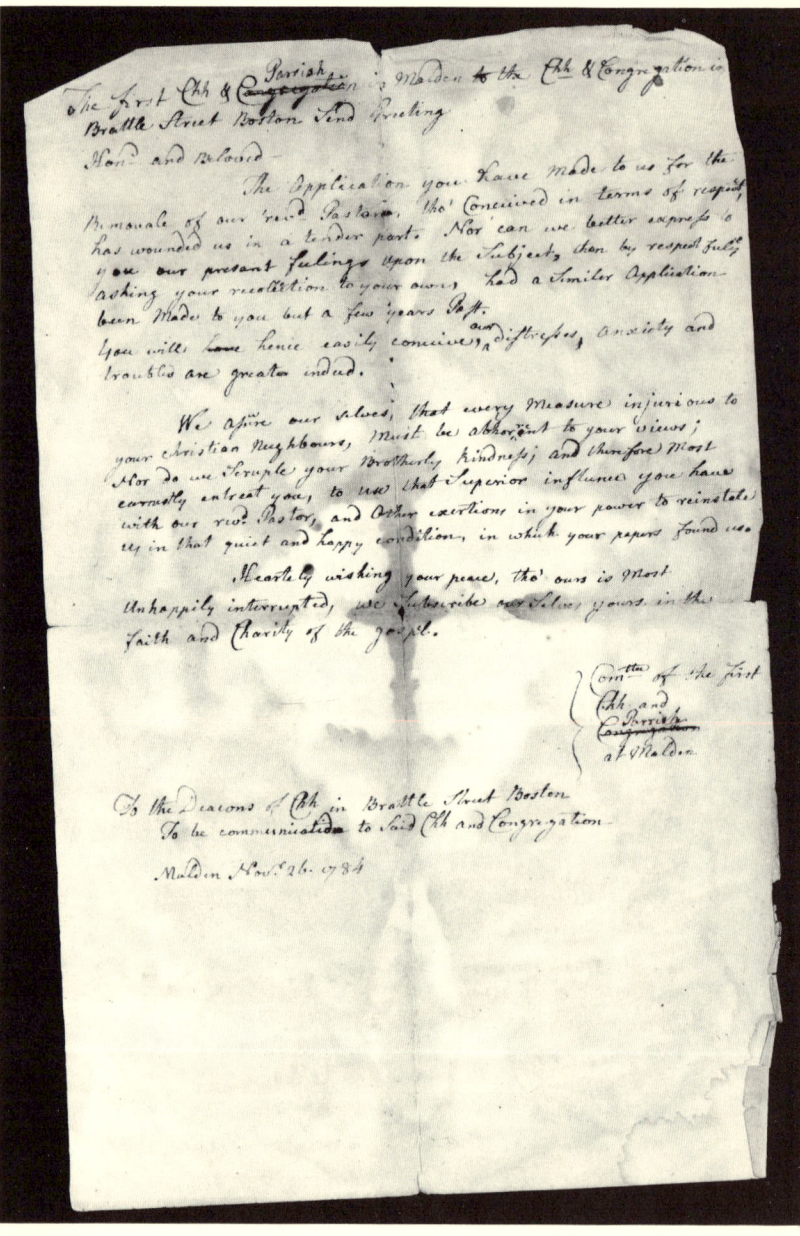

Letter from the Committee of the First Church of Malden to the Brattle Street Church in Boston protesting the transfer of Reverend Peter Thacher, "the young Elijah," to the Boston parish in 1784.

Civic Protection to Date

As of the fall of 1973 Malden continued to be well protected by both its police and firemen. The latest figure showed 118 men in the Police Department with squads designated as traffic, juvenile, liquor and vice, as well as the regular police force. A Canine Unit continues to be effective with its three police officers, each in charge of a well trained police dog. New police quarters are under construction in the developing Government Civic Center where this department will eventually be located, hopefully by 1975. At the present time 166 firemen serve the city. Five fire stations, located in strategic sections of the city, have eleven modern pieces of equipment. No new stations have been built since the Central Station on Salem and Sprague Streets was opened. Others are located on Pearl Street in the Edgeworth district, Ashland Street on Belmont Hill, Laurel Street in Maplewood and Oliver Street in Linden. The Malden Civil Defense Unit occupies the old Mountain Avenue Fire Station.

Churches and Synagogues

Protestant churches, Catholic parishes, and synagogues remain active within the city. First Church, Congregational remains on Pleasant Street, next to the new Government Civic Center. Centre United Methodist and Robinson United Methodist united in 1973 and the parishioners worship in their completed new structure, built on the previous Centre Church location, Pleasant and Washington Streets. St. Paul's Episcopal Church is on Washington Street and St. Luke's Episcopal in Linden. First Parish, Universalist is at 2 Elm Street, Mystic Side, Congregational, on Main Street just over the Malden line in Everett. Emmanuel Baptist Church is at the corner of Hillside and Eastern Avenue, Church of God at the corner of Appleton and Main Streets. The First Church of The Nazarene occupies its new structure at 529 Eastern Avenue which was dedicated in 1973. First Church of Christ, Scientist is at Main and Spring Streets, First Baptist Church in Converse Square, and Forestdale Community Church at Gordon and Forest Streets. In Maplewood the Maplewood Baptist is at the corner of Salem and Church Streets, Maplewood Congregational at 557 Salem Street, First Lutheran on Waite and Church Streets, Christ United Methodist, corner of Salem and Webster Streets, and Kingdom Hall on Salem Street.

Catholic Churches are located as follows: Sacred Hearts at 315

Main Street; St. Joseph's at 796 Salem Street; St. Peter's, corner of Pearl and Thacher Streets; Immaculate Conception, Fellsway and Pleasant Street. One Mass is held each Sunday at the Oak Grove Community Center, Oak Grove Square, offered by the Immaculate Conception Church.

Synagogues include Congregation Beth Israel West, Orthodox, 10 Dexter Street, and Beth Israel East, Orthodox, Cross & Faulkner Streets; Young Israel of Malden, Orthodox, 45 Holyoke Street; Congregation Agudas Achim, Conservative, 160 Harvard Street; Temple Ezrath Israel, Conservative, 245 Bryant Street; Temple Tifereth Israel, Reform, 539 Salem Street.

Organization Housing

Twenty-five years after World War II the face of Malden has changed drastically. Religious leaders backed by their parishioners pledged their help to overcome the blighted conditions. Housing became the foremost project in the determined effort of several religious faiths. Salem Towers, corner of Pierce and Salem Streets, was sponsored by a group of men from Beth Israel. When the nine-story Salem Towers was built with its eighty apartments for the elderly with moderate income, it was the city's tallest structure. Agudas Achim sponsored construction of a hundred garden-type apartments for moderate income families in the former Suffolk Square area.

Early in 1971 upper Pleasant Street became the focal point for redevelopment. Under the sponsorship of First Church a 209 unit apartment house of nine stories for senior citizens of 62 years of age and older with moderate income, was built across Pleasant Street, opposite First Church. The cornerstone laying took place on October 13th that year, occupancy began in January, 1972. Incorporated on May 10, 1968, under a governing committee called First Church in Malden Homes, Inc., the apartment building, named "The Heritage," provided a convenient resident location in the downtown section of the city.

Newman Towers, on Newman Road, two blocks from Main Street in the Belmont Hill section, was Malden's first condominium, opening on October 7, 1973.

First Church, Congregational, continues to provide rooms for instruction of those children whose learning process is impaired, following the schedule of public school sessions. From the spring of 1971 to May, 1974, First Church made accommodations available for

Architect's rendering of "The Heritage," 209-unit apartment for senior citizens built with federal funds under the sponsorship of the First Church, Congregational.

noontime lunches for the elderly. Thereafter, the program returned to Centre Methodist Church where it had been held before the church fire in 1971. The apartment housing for the elderly at 630 Salem Street in Maplewood and at 120 Mountain Avenue, opposite Malden Armory, are two other convenient lunch centers. A fourth location for the city's noontime hot lunch program opened on June 17, 1974, in the Immaculate Conception Church Parish Hall, corner of Highland Avenue and Charles Street, to accommodate residents on the west side of the city. These meals served at a cost of 50c are provided by Malden Action Home Care, Inc. They cost Malden $1.25 per meal, the difference being covered by a government subsidy, and are for the benefit of those persons sixty years and over.

First Baptist Church operates a Senior Citizens Community Drop-in Center; First Parish, Universalist has a Thursday West End Drop-in Center.

An AcID (Adolescent Counselling in Development) Center, an agency for young people in trouble in Malden, Medford and Everett, opened in the late 1960's when the drug problem caused serious concern for authorities and citizens at large. A program was undertaken by a Malden priest, Father Bernard Lane with headquarters in a house on Linden Avenue adjacent to Pleasant Street. Later it moved to 170 Pleasant Street in the second-story rooms of a building east of First Church. Project Genesis was conducted by volunteers for a few years in St. Paul's Episcopal Church, its most active period having been between 1968 and 1972.

There is also a "meals-on-wheels" program for shut-ins. The latest benefit for the elderly, "Project Senior Citizen" discount card program, begun in December, 1974, and sponsored jointly by the Malden Action Home Care and the Chamber of Commerce, has been enthusiastically received. By the first of January, 1975, the registration exceeded the one thousand mark with over thirty firms cooperating.

As previously mentioned the Women's Christian Temperance Union which was organized in 1874 had served as one of the community's leading groups in the area of social reform. Although its members had accomplished much good, undoubtedly the changing social climate of the Post World War II years contributed to its eventual disappearance from Malden.

Malden's Religious Life Today

By 1960, Malden had a very vigorous Protestant church membership with over twenty-five churches representing ten denominations. Three Catholic Churches and St. Peter's Mission were caring for the parishioners of that faith. Several Jewish Temples were situated in the eastern section, one on the west side of the city. A few other religious sects had been started.

For a time, the Covenant Congregational and Swedish Congregational congregations were active. With changing conditions, the church building at the corner of Lebanon and Granite Streets, where both religious societies met, was remodeled into an apartment house.

Emmanuel Baptist Church was formed in 1946 when the Eastern Avenue and Union Baptist Churches merged. Its present building was the location of the Unitarian Church of earlier years. On May 22, 1838, First Parish, Universalist, was formally organized. The present edifice at 2 Elm Street was begun in 1907 with the first service held there in 1909. First Baptist Church built its present structure at Main and Salem Streets in 1915 after fire destroyed an earlier building. The two earliest meeting places were on Salem Street along what was then known as Baptist Row. The two magnificent stained glass windows, a gift from the Honorable Alvin T. Fuller, which enhance the sanctuary of the present Main Street structure are impressive and notable works of religious art. They were designed by Charles J. Connick and were dedicated in April, 1941.

The Methodists dedicated their first church building April 27,

1826. The second edifice, built at the corner of Waverly and Pleasant Streets, was ready for services in 1842. The red brick structure, a block west on Pleasant Street, was begun in 1871 and dedicated on May 13, 1874. A fire destroyed the hundred year old Centre Church on May 16, 1971. Formal consecration of a new building erected on the same site took place on February 24th, 1974. Robinson United Methodist Church merged with Centre Church on June 1, 1973. However, the parishioners continued to hold services in their Belmont Hill building until Centre Church was completed. Centre Church held services and activities in neighboring St. Paul's Episcopal Church during the construction of the new edifice.

Changing trends and attitudes toward religion as well as population changes necessitated some churches combining with others of like denomination in the eastern section of the city. The Swedish Methodist Church merged with Maplewood Methodist, Linden Methodist, and Faulkner Methodist Churches to become Christ United Methodist Church. A modern building was constructed in 1967 on the site of the Swedish Methodist Church, corner of Webster and Salem Streets. Linden Congregational Church was closed in 1970 with final services held on Easter Sunday. Many of these parishioners joined First Church, Congregational.

A united celebration of worship held on a spring Sunday of 1973 officially marked the merger of Centre and Robinson United Methodist Churches. The observance was held in the Belmont Hill Church, corner of Boston and Fairmont Streets. It was stated that "this union brings together a history of 152 years of Centre Church and 91 years of Robinson and its predecessor, the Belmont Union Church." The parish hall in the new center building was named the Robinson Memorial Fellowship Hall to preserve the Robinson name and to commemorate the merger.

After its founding in 1898, the Christian Science Church met in various halls in Malden until the first unit of the present church was built in 1921 at the corner of Spring and Main Streets. Five years later, the church was completed.

First Church of the Nazarene, formerly located in Judson Square, celebrated its fiftieth anniversary there. When fire destroyed that building the location was abandoned and the congregation met in a vacant church building on Salem Street until 1972 when the new structure was completed at 529 Eastern Avenue in the urban renewal area. On Sunday, October 7, 1973, the parishioners dedicated two church buses in order to reach members in outlying areas and contact the unchurched families in the immediate church area.

The First Evangelical Lutheran Church on Waite Street has been active for many years and continues to reach its communicants in Malden and surrounding towns.

The non-denominational Calvary Temple on Myrtle Street started with seven people in 1954 and continued to grow for a time. Malden had a congregation of Jehovah's Witnesses which became active in the city in 1938 and was located at 170 Pleasant Street. A new building, Kingdom Hall, was later erected on Salem Street about opposite Pierce Street.

Forestdale Community Church, corner of Forest and Gordon Streets, still meets in the former chapel built during the latter part of 1892. Modernized and kept in good repair, it has filled a great need in that section since it was built under the sponsorship of First Church after several months of group prayer meetings and Sunday School sessions held in a private home on Mt. Vernon Street. It became an independent church after forty years of support by its parent denomination.

First Church, Congregational, built its eighth and present colonial church in 1934 (with dedication the next year) on the site of the former gothic structure, which was destroyed by fire on December 13, 1933. Its previous building in Malden Square had been blown down by the September gale of 1869.

St. Paul's Episcopal Church on Washington Street continues to be active and is still at its original site since it was organized as Grace Church. The first service was held on September 30, 1861, in a private home. Because of its growing membership a hall called "Good Templars' Hall," was secured over a store in Hill's Building located on the northerly side of Irving Street. On October 17, 1861, a group of ten persons formed the Grace Church Episcopal Society and met in the hall over the waiting room and ticket office of the original Boston and Maine Railroad Station.

Twenty years later St. Luke's Episcopal Church was formed in Linden at the junction of Lynn Street and Eastern Avenue.

From a population of 6,840 in 1865 to 38,037 in 1905, an immediate need was expressed by many Malden residents for another Catholic church for parishioners in the central and eastern sections of the city. Father Thomas Shahan, referred to as "The Church Builder" because of the many churches he had built in the diocese, was assigned the task of building the new edifice. The large brick structure on Main Street, Sacred Hearts Church, opened for its first Mass on May 6, 1892. This Church proved to be the last and finest of the churches Father Shahan built. Previous to the new building's erection, Masses were held for the first year and a half in the Malden Opera House at 454 North Main Street, the location now occupied by Kotzen's Furniture Store.

In 1883 Mr. and Mrs. John B. Faulkner gave the land and building for the Evangelical Union Church which had been meeting in Mystic Hall in Faulkner. It was from this beginning that the Faulkner Methodist Church came into existence, erecting a building at the corner of Salem and Pierce Streets. In the 1960's this building was purchased by the Square and Compass Club of the Masonic Lodges in Malden, and provided a meeting place for its members until the spring of 1974.

In his *Ecclesiastical History* published in 1890 by the Rev. Joshua W. Wellman, D.D., pastor of the Trinitarian (later First) Congregational Church from 1874 to 1883, he said: "With all their imperfections, mistakes, and partial failures, they (the churches) have stood as the bulwark against immorality, intemperance, all unrighteousness and crime. Without churches and the preached gospel, Malden would have been uninhabitable to respectable people. They have been the light, the joy, and the glory of the town."

In 1922 it was decided to sell the Edgeworth Chapel, dedicated in 1866 and maintained by the parishioners of First Church, Congregational to assist the Italian people who had migrated to this section. First Church had constructed a new Parish House adjacent to the Church. It was anticipated that the children in the Edgeworth district would attend the First Church Sunday School and join with the youth there in various activities. Such was not the case, however. On November 11, 1923, the Edgeworth Chapel was purchased by the Catholic diocese and became known thereafter as St. Peter's Mission, and was principally for the Italian residents in that neighborhood. On October 27, 1973, the Mission became the fourth Catholic parish in Malden. A renovated building at the corner of Pearl and Thacher Streets and seating about 350 continues to serve the Italian people in that section of the city.

St. Joseph's Church in Maplewood was built at its present site when the new parish was founded March 15, 1902. The present building standing adjacent to the parish school is a beautiful structure erected in 1962. In the western section of Malden, the original Immaculate Conception Catholic Church was razed and a modern structure was built during 1963 and 1964 on the same site. The dedication was held on November 21, 1964. The building has been acclaimed for its architectural appointments.

Since 1943 when Mrs. Alfred Avery became its first president,

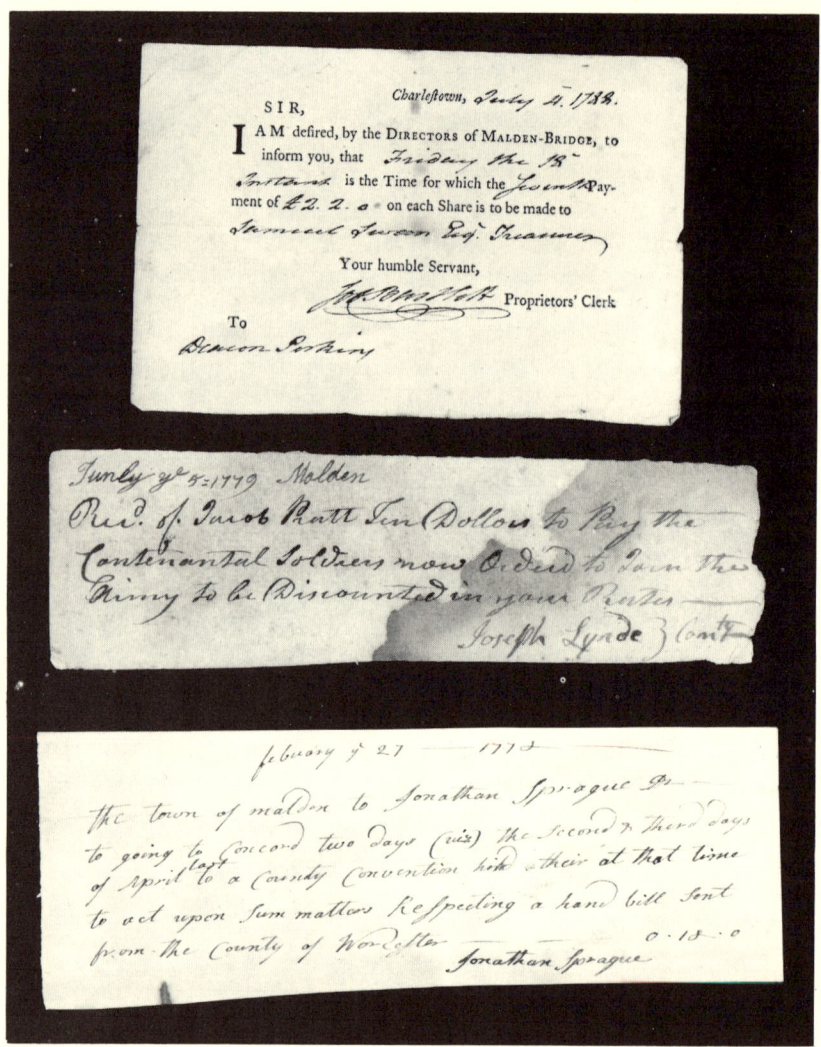

(Top) Dividend notice of the Malden Bridge dated July 4, 1788, successor a year earlier to the Penny Ferry established in 1640.

(Center) Receipt to Jacob Pratt dated July 5, 1779, for ten dollars "to pay the Continental Soldiers now ordered to join the Army . . ."

(Bottom) Bill to the Town of Malden from Jonathan Sprague dated February 27, 1772, for expenses ". . . to going to Concord two days . . . to a County Convention . . ."

Church Women United has flourished in Malden. Between fifteen and seventeen churches as well as the Salvation Army and the YWCA have participated in the yearly general and state council programs. Ten years before Malden Council came into being (1933), a yearly Day of Prayer was observed with representative church women in attendance at the invitation of the officers of Malden Y.W.C.A. To date eleven presidents have represented ten different churches.

Schooling

The Forestdale School on Sylvan Street was built to replace the old wooden Ayers primary building on Cherry Street. The Daniels School was named for Charles A. Daniels, Malden High School headmaster (1862-1884). The Maplewood School, built in 1962 on Broadway, became a Junior High School, named in memory of Marcia P. Browne, principal of the former Maplewood School which became a primary school. The new building was erected on the same site as a previous one. The Chester W. Holmes School, named for the school superintendent who served from 1946 to 1961, was built to cover the entire block between Tremont and Mt. Vernon Streets and Mountain Avenue. It replaced the Pierce School that had stood on a portion of this area for many years. With the growth of Ward 6 in Linden, schools were required in that section. Because of the development of the urban renewal area a new Linden School was built to accommodate the growing number of children. The Maplewood and Glenwood Schools each had additions constructed to handle the larger enrollments.

The Immaculate Conception Parish was the birthplace of parochial education in the city. The first red brick school built on the north corner of Highland Avenue and Charles Street in 1881, introduced the School Sisters of Notre Dame to the area. That first year there were nine Sisters and about 450 pupils. The second school was opened in 1891. Girl's Catholic High School, founded in 1908, originally occupied the third story of the grammar school, popularly known as "the Red School." The new high school was started in 1922. The next year students and faculty moved to their new building on the West Street side of the school yard. The noted "Red School" was within recent years named Monsignor Donovan Parish Hall in recognition of the pastor who was at one time in charge of St. Peter's Mission Church. Girl's Catholic was the only parochial school among seven in the nation selected to conduct a United Nations Education, Scientific,

Cultural Organization program. During the project, many internationally known celebrities from the United Nations General Assembly visited the Malden school.

A high school for boys was built in 1927. On November 11, 1945, the old grammar school for boys was destroyed by fire. Immediately a new building was built and was dedicated on July 6, 1947. The Xaverian Brothers staffed the Boy's High School, starting in 1952. The Highland Avenue building has a cornerstone date of 1931.

The Sacred Hearts parish purchased from the Universalists the brick church then standing on Main Street opposite the Catholic church, and converted it into classrooms. The last parish meeting of the Universalists was held in the building on July 22, 1908. The Catholic school opened with four rooms for classes. Extension of the car line through Malden and the necessity to straighten that section of Main Street, caused the school property to be taken by eminent domain in 1909. New property was purchased on the north side of Irving Street, near Ferry Street, for a schoolhouse. Here the brick Cheverus Centennial School with eighteen rooms was erected and opened in the fall of 1908. The Sisters of Providence taught at this school. A fine marble bust of Cardinal Cheverus was erected above the top of the facade with the dates "1808-1908" inscribed below the school name. The Cheverus School Hall, with a combination gymnasium and assembly hall, was erected adjoining the brick school, its cornerstone dated A.D. 1965, and occupancy taking place in October. The former Centre Grammar School stood on this location.

Erected in 1950, St. Joseph's School on Salem Street, adjacent to the parish church in Maplewood, was opened. The latest school to be built, Malden Catholic High School, erected on a section of urban renewal land off Broadway on Crystal Street in a lower section of Maplewood near the Everett line, opened in September, 1968.

School Activities–1974

The 117th annual commencement ceremony for the 635 members of the Senior Class of Malden High School was held, June 5, 1974, at Macdonald Stadium on Pearl Street. Outdoor exercises for this afternoon program had been customary for many years. Previously, Gay Auditorium in the older section, then Jenkins Auditorium in the newer addition of the High School, were the scenes of evening commencements until such time as the number of graduates exceeded the convenience and popularity for audience attendance. As an interesting comparison, the 1974 graduating high school class exceeded the entire enrollment of the student body when the high school opened in 1899 to accommodate its five hundred students.

Nineteen seventy-four marked the fifth year for the progressive seven-week Title I federally-funded program under the Education Act. This funding enabled Malden to arrange sessions in five schools: Emerson, Leonard, Daniels, Lincoln and Linden, to accommodate the three hundred children who participated. Since its inception the program had developed considerably and become popular with both children and parents, especially since the scope of its many benefits were better understood. The fifth year's sessions involved a corps of assistants under the supervision of a director including: eleven teachers, twenty-two student aides, twenty-two parental aides, three testers, three speech therapists, two counselors, two nurses and two language specialists. With educators more keenly aware of the limitations and needs of many children from low-income sections of the city, the expanded schedule provided welcome aid and constructive advancement. In addition to a play and learning process, educational and physical tests as well as behavorial criteria have better prepared and encouraged pre-school children to adjust to the complexities of early school life.

Changing Aspects

Fancy balls, banquets, receptions, and lengthy parades were enjoyed during the 1920's and continued at a slower pace during the Depression until World War II. With all the complexities of the war years, the long hours of work, and household upheavals, the elaborate events and formal affairs of earlier years were never renewed. In many respects life changed for most Americans as traditional home restrictions and discipline were greatly relaxed. Attitudes of returning war veterans changed as did those of many Americans who worked for the first time during the war. It was a prelude to the immense changes in morals, manners, and behavior to come during the 1960's and 1970's.

Since 1967 the entire country was affected by the small but vocal percentage of young people who rebelled against the Vietnam War. Disorders of a destructive nature caused concern and serious problems to those in positions of leadership. The extent of drug use and addiction became alarming. Malden was as affected as other communities with upheaval, destruction of property, and lack of obedience to law and order. Moral standards dropped to an all-time low while permissiveness brought problems for law enforcement agencies. "Drop-in Centers" were established to improve conditions among the young people affected by drugs and unable to cope with various problems.

The conclusion of the Vietnam War, the return of the POWS, and the easing of the draft for young men, brought improvement. The outlook of many young people changed. Fewer "marches" were held. More constructive methods of publicizing their objection to "the establishment" drew less attention. With the voting age lowered to eighteen it was hoped that young people would become interested and active in government. However, the upheaval in Washington politics and Watergate only disgusted and antagonzied the new voters.

Construction and Face-Lifting

During the week of September 9, 1973, the first phase of the projected 1,021 apartment units, known as Granada Highlands in Linden, was officially opened. This large scale apartment community was developed on a forty-acre elevated site off Route C-1 on Malden's Linden Highlands plateau as part of the Malden Redevelopment Authority renewal project. This $50 million complex includes a clubhouse with areas for sports and crafts, as well as rooms where residents can hold functions.

Delays necessitated by a court order retarded the building of the Howard W. Fitzpatrick housing project in the area of Pleasant and Vista Streets close by the Fellsway. By spring of 1974 work was underway and the project was completed for occupancy by January, 1975.

The beginning of a $26 million renovation of the upper Pleasant Street area began in 1972 with the razing of all buildings beyond The Heritage on the north side, and from First Church, Congregational, on the south side of Pleasant Street as far as the railroad bridge beyond Florence Street. This thruway was widened and housing on the south side was razed beyond St. Paul's Episcopal Church on the corner of Florence and Washington Streets. An additional parking lot back of the Church and other parking areas in the center of the city became necessary to encourage business and draw people to the downtown area.

Apartment housing for the elderly on Salem Street, near Maplewood Square, a similar type structure on Mountain Avenue, and the privately owned King's View apartment complex on Pierce Street, in

Architect's rendering of new City Hall and Civic Center scheduled for completion in May, 1975.

Forestdale, have added greatly to Malden's face-lifting during 1973 and 1974.

On the morning of June 1, 1973, ground-breaking ceremonies were held at the site of the long awaited Civic (City Hall) Center to be erected in the block where the Strand Theatre and a block of stores had stood, encompassing Pleasant, Abbott, Commercial, and Exchange Streets. The parking lot belonging to First Church and Abbott Street disappeared as demolition got underway in the spring of 1973.

Malden's new seven-story City Hall-Government Civic Center, estimated to cost more than $8 million when completed and furnished, began to rise with its foundation and steel work well advanced by the dawn of 1974. Its completion was contemplated for May, 1975. The new complex includes a police station and garage with egress onto Exchange Street. Space for federal and state government agency offices, as well as city offices, and frontage for small commercial stores also are planned. Built of red brick, the building will meet the long awaited need for a new City Hall. Hopefully a park with shops, covered mall, and condominiums will improve the area adjacent to the east side of First Church.

The years 1973-74 and early 1975 saw the demolition of buildings following the course of Commercial Street to Medford Street. Pleasant Street buildings southwest beyond the railroad bridge to Pearl Street were razed before 1974 arrived. This entire area has become a renewal

Rebirth

project of great magnitude. Drawing board plans are waiting financial arrangements for construction to start.

With the extension of the MBTA rapid transit line through Malden and a new station beyond the Civic Center, plans have been completed for further improvements and construction begun. The Boston & Maine Railroad corporation sold its seventeen miles of right-of-way between Boston and Reading to the Massachusetts Bay Transportation Company, to serve for the MBTA's projected rapid transit line. New tracks between Boston and Oak Grove to the Melrose line are scheduled to be completed in 1975. Budd cars have been operating the commuter service for many years. By the beginning of 1974 adjacent sections of housing in Oak Grove and other necessary land had been cleared in preparation for the new rapid transit line.

In January, 1974, a $4 million Pine Banks Park recreational development plan was unveiled. This development of the 152 acre site was proposed by Frank McHugh, a landscape architect and horticulturist and a member of the Malden Planning Board staff. If such a huge undertaking should be approved by the joint Commission of Malden and Melrose, it would be the first massive redevelopment of the park in a century.

Vietnam War

On August 2, 1964, the longest war in United States history was ignited by an incident in the Gulf of Tonkin when an American destroyer patrolling off the North Vietnam coast was attacked by three torpedo boats.

Many Malden men served in the long struggle with sixteen killed during the eight years. These included ten who served in the Army and six Marines, with a complete list in preparation as this book went to press.

Space Age

After years of study, development and experiment, America's space age took form. On May 5, 1961, Alan B. Shepard took a suborbital, 15-minute flight aboard *Freedom 7* to inaugurate the decade of manned flights in space. His flight which started the Mercury Program proved successful. On February 20, 1962, Lieutenant Colonel John H. Glenn, Jr. became the first United States astronaut to orbit the earth, and on Christmas Eve of 1968, three American astronauts circled the moon in *Apollo 8*. On July 20, 1969, the world watched TV in awed wonder as Neil Armstrong climbed out of his Apollo 16 lunar module and stepped onto the moon's surface to relay his historic message, "That's one small step for man, one giant leap for mankind." Armstrong and his companion ("Buzz") Edwin Aldrin, planted an American flag and erected a plaque there which had inscribed upon its surface: "Here men from the planet Earth first set foot upon the moon, July, 1969 A.D. We came in peace for all mankind." The country had come a long way since December 17, 1903, when the Wright brothers' airplane took off at Kitty Hawk and managed to stay in the air for fifty-nine seconds. On February 8, 1974, the three astronauts parachuted their Apollo ferry ship into the Pacific Ocean in perfect form after eighty-four days aboard the orbiting space station, *Skylab 3*. This crew's return ended an era of manned space exploration by the United States, man's longest space mission.

Advances in the Last Decade

In the decade from 1963 through 1973 science and technology have made great strides including the introduction of open-heart surgery which, although not without its failures, has successfully extended the life span of many people, and made advances in treating cancer and other diseases.

Technologically computers have become commonplace in business and industrial operations. Many new products like the snowmobile have been introduced for winter sport fans. Satellite communications systems have been developed and since 1965 have carried television around the world.

The Clean Air Act of 1963, with amendments in 1965 and again in 1970, sought to reduce pollution in every form. Pollution of rivers, even the ocean, land and air was a critical problem during the 1960's and continues today. Attempts through rigid regulations and laws of federal and state governments are focusing on corrective action but progress is slow in achieving any definite goal. Malden has joined the project.

Cable TV was introduced in Malden in the late 1960's. It was the first city in the Boston area to adopt the cablevision system, permitting the selection of two additional channels for viewing local programs. Those desiring this extra service were required to pay for the privilege and special wiring was required for such installations.

In the 1960's the "women's liberation" crusade began to take

Davenport Memorial Home, originally built as his residence in 1892 by A. H. Davenport, renowned custom furniture maker.

shape and focused on equal rights for women. By 1973 this movement had headlined programs of various kinds, emphasizing the latest in women's advancement as it ventured into almost every phase of public life.

The 26th Amendment became effective in 1971 and gave American citizens eighteen years or older the right to vote. The elderly began receiving medicare amd medicaid benefits. The birth control pill has been accepted but still causes discussions on a scientific level as well as being questioned by lay people on a religious level. Kidney transplants have been developed to a high degree. More accurate weather forecasting has made life easier with its advanced science.

Drugs have been blamed for the increase of violence, with law enforcement at a low ebb. Assassination of a President and two prominent figures within a short span of years shocked a saddened nation. Campus riots and "freedom" marches against anything or everything by a minority of radicals and restless, frustrated youth, brought thoughts and fears of "a national sickness." By 1974 the country was calmer.

When President Nixon spoke on TV on November 7, 1973, he outlined the several difficulties involved in a nation-wide energy crisis. "The country," he said, "was heading toward the most acute shortages of energy since World War II." He affirmed that there would be less energy available, less heat, less electricity, less gasoline. Thermostats must be lowered to 68° and speed limit of cars and trucks lowered to 55 miles per hour. On November 13, 1973, Governor Francis Sargent announced fuel conservation measures. Under a new energy-saving law signed by President Nixon on January 6, 1974, daylight saving would become a year-round requirement to be observed for the next two years. The law was amended and four months of Standard Time resumed, October 27, 1974.

Under the Emergency Highway Conservation Act all states were pressured to establish the 55 mile per hour speed limit effective January 6, 1974. Unless states complied future federal aid for highway construction would be withheld. There appeared to be signs of "the end of abundance." By the winter of 1974 shortages in fuel oil and gasoline were creating nation-wide problems such as the loss of business and laying off of help, both provoking severe repercussions.

Prominent Citizens and Foundations

One of Malden's prominent citizens was Deloraine P. Corey, historian and author of the only authoritative source of Malden's history and covering the English background through the city's growth to 1785. He spent forty-five years in its compilation and prepared many brief sketches on Malden's history for publication during the city's several earlier observances. He had the assistance of his son (who died in 1891 when only twenty-five) in compiling the information on the gravestones in Malden's earliest cemetery, Bell Rock, a painstaking accomplishment which is now filed in the Malden Public Library.

John A. Volpe, well known in Malden where he established a construction business, served as Governor of Massachusetts for three terms, bringing honor to Malden. He was commissioner of public works for Massachusetts and federal highway administrator for President Eisenhower. He served more than six years as governor before resigning to accept the cabinet post of Secretary of Transportation when Mr. Nixon assumed the presidency. After Mr. Nixon's reelection in November, 1972, Mr. Volpe was appointed ambassador to Italy with residence in Rome where he is still holding this post.

Alvan Tufts Fuller, a Malden resident, served two terms as Governor of Massachusetts. As a youth he sold bicycles and developed a business ability which enabled him to become one of the leading merchants in the country in the automobile trade. In Boston he built up the largest automobile dealership and headquarters in the state. He

Senior citizen housing at Cross and Willow Streets, completed in July, 1966.

served in the United States House of Representatives in 1915 and in 1916 was elected to the sixty-fifth Congress for two terms. He served as Lieutenant Governor before ascending to the highest office in Massachusetts. Mr. Fuller returned uncashed all the salary checks he received in the many offices he had held.

Mrs. Albert Schofield, more familiarly known as Judge Emma, is one of the city's most distinguished and best known residents. Quoting from a published article of some years past we learn that among her numerous accomplishments, "she was the first woman named to the bench in New England, the first woman Assistant Attorney General, first of her sex to serve as a probation officer in Western Massachusetts." In 1930, Judge Schofield was appointed Associate Justice of the Malden District Court, an official position which she held until her retirement in 1957. She is a direct descendant of Ralph Sprague who was an early settler in Malden and prominent citizen.

In 1914 William G. Willcox, then living in New York, gave his father's house at the corner of Linden and Mountain Avenues for a home for girls and a social center. A corporation was formed on January 16, 1915, as The Girls' Club Association of Malden, Inc. with a Board of Directors and Trustees to supervise the home known as Willcox Hall. This association was an outgrowth of the Enterprise Club composed of young women from First Church, Congregational, who conducted social service work at the Edgeworth Chapel on Pearl Street for the benefit of the Italian families who settled in that area.

The Malden Home for Aged Persons was established by prominent men in the community. Malden YWCA was formed to encourage social and civic groups among young women within a community

Modern plant of Berkshire Apparel Corporation at Middlesex and Charles Streets, typical of Malden's newer industrial buildings, opened July, 1966.

center. Headquarters continue to be located in the former Ramsdell home of one of Malden's well-known families.

Two foundations have been most beneficial to the city. One, the Adelaide Breed Bayrd Foundation, was established and incorporated on December 13, 1927, with generous contributions donated yearly on the birthday anniversary of Mrs. Bayrd, as specified by a governing board. The Davenport Memorial Foundation was established on April 2, 1946, as the result of a bequest under the will of Miss Alice M. Davenport, following her death in 1944. She left her beautiful and spacious family home, built in 1892 by her father, Albert H. Davenport, for a retirement home for Malden couples whose qualifications are approved by a board of trustees. A yearly portion of the foundation's income is donated to various organizations within the city.

Patient Care for the Elderly

For the last quarter of this century, nursing homes have become an essential part of the community life. At least ten such facilities were operating in the West End section until restrictions necessitated the closing of a few of the homes. The large older-type houses in this section of the city had provided suitable arrangements for patient care and required facilities, and today seven are in operation. Year by year more stringent regulations were demanded by the government when federal funding was offered for substantial assistance.

Originally opened as the privately owned Maplewood Hospital, the institution later became Webster Manor Nursing Home in the Maplewood section.

Maplewood apartments for senior citizens on Salem Street with accommodations for 217 persons, opened in April, 1973.

The former Contagious Hospital in Forestdale which was owned by the city continues as another nursing home in that area. There is one other facility in the southern section of Malden, the Dexter House on Main Street, south of Bell Rock Park. It is the only such facility built strictly for the nursing of sick and convalescent patients. With hospitals overcrowded as a rule, such nursing homes become a haven for the elderly who require and crave comfort and kindly care.

Sustaining Groups Within the City

A large number of organizations and societies, some small, others of greater numbers, continues to flourish as would be expected in a city the size of Malden. Some provide sociability for the membership, others have charitable goals as a purposeful means of sustaining interest. Fraternal bodies, veterans' organizations, patriotic societies, civic and social groups for adults and the younger generation, have held in the past and assuredly continue to hold an estimable place

124-unit apartment for senior citizens on Mountain Avenue was completed in March, 1972.

within the "heartbeat" of the city. Those who have been residents for a long period of time can no doubt remember groups which have since dissolved and whose earlier activities seem now but a faded memory. It is true and understandably so, that many groups and organizations have felt a change of interest and lack of growth since the coming of television. The shift in population can account for some of the diminishing enthusiasm in almost all groups. Possibly time will reverse this trend.

Bicentennial Plans Begun

The anticipation of "The Bicentennial of '76" was the theme of President Nixon's second inaugural parade, with floats and banners accenting it. When the President spoke on TV to open the Bicentennial, he outlined several ideas including establishment of a commission to bring plans into focus. The celebration was to cover the lengthy heritage from the beginning at Jamestown to the moon landings, with an assessment of the nation's major achievements. Each state and most cities or towns would plan individual celebrations fitting for the occasion.

Boston opened the celebration with a reenactment of the Boston Tea Party on that event's 200th Anniversary, December 16, 1973. Malden joined in this anniversary with publicity in the *Malden Evening News* on the Friday previous to the celebration, outlining the part Malden took both before and at the time of the Boston Tea Party. As previously stated notable statements were written by the minister of Malden at that time, the Rev. Peter Thacher, an active patriot and respected young pastor who guided the town through the long years of the Revolutionary War.

With the recreated Boston Tea Party plans appeared to be in the formative stage for a nation-wide day of humiliation, fasting, and prayer, as proposed by Senator Mark Hatfield and his colleagues. It will be remembered that "on May 24, 1774, under the sponsorship of Thomas Jefferson, Patrick Henry, and others, the Virginia Assembly passed a resolution calling for a 'day of fasting, humiliation and prayer' as a show of solidarity with their fellow countrymen of Boston."

The underlying purpose of this special day was to accent the fact that June 1, 1974, would mark the two hundredth anniversary of the closing of the port of Boston by the British in response to the refusal by Boston and neighboring towns to pay for the tea dumped from the three cargo ships into Boston Harbor on December 16, 1773. Malden responded quite forcibly to this British disciplinary action, the response having been recorded within these pages under the Revolutionary War.

With public aknowledgement regarding Malden's action to the Boston Tea Party in the *Malden Evening News* of December 14, 1973, prepared from a script written by the compiler of this history, the bicentennial celebration started on its way in Malden. This anniversary has been further advanced by articles written by the First Church historian and printed in the First Church "CORNERSTONE" beginning with the September, 1973, issue.

With the bicentennial events anticipated over the next two years, First Church, Congregational, and First Parish, Universalist, celebrated the 325th anniversary of the gathering of Malden's earliest religious Meeting House on Bell Rock which became Malden's birthplace for both its religious and civic life. Thus, the establishment of the town of Malden was made possible by the gathering of a church which had to be organized before a town could be incorporated.

Acknowledgment of this significant occasion culminated in varied observances during early 1974 through the first week in May, which was the official date duly recorded for Malden's religious beginnings. Both denominations celebrated the event, both having been one in the Congregational faith for almost two centuries.

Under the chairmanship of Colonel Walter T. Anzoni, U.S.A.R., Retired, as this book goes to press, Malden's Bicentennial Commission's plans call for an evening's entertainment by the U.S. Navy Band, a colonial dinner and ball to be held in the new Civic Center, a street parade, a program for Flag Day, and a bus tour of houses. Activities are being coordinated so that all participating organizations will work under this one committee. Thus these city-wide observances will be meaningful and significantly related to the nation's 200th Anniversary.

Years Yet to Come

"The science of government of municipalities, as indeed of all government, is becoming more complex, the problems more difficult each year. Each year is a new adventure and demands new methods and new ideas." This statement is as true in 1974 as in January of 1924—fifty years ago, when it was delivered at the inauguration of the Mayor of Malden and the city government. That year marked the 275th anniversary of the incorporation of the town, then called "Maulden." It was further stated that same night of inauguration that, "in all our 275 years of history I doubt if there has been a greater change or a more

Rebirth

The official Town Seal of Malden at the left, adapted from the arms of the Borough of Maldon, England, was supplanted by the official City Seal at the right early in 1882.

interesting one than we witness tonight in the advent of women welcomed into membership in our Common Council. They have equal titles, equal privileges, equal rights, equal votes, equal voice and must sustain equal burdens and responsibilities."

The Mayor closed that address by stating:

"The success of each year's administration depends on, unitedly, striving always for 'whatsoever things are honest, whatsoever things are just, whatsoever things are pure . . . whatsoever things are of good report.' In this spirit, appreciative and grateful for her great past, yet looking steadfastly toward those years yet to come, whose number we may not count, let us approach our great task in a spirit of mutual forbearance, of generosity, and of helpfulness, ever keeping before us a high ideal of service to this old, yet ever new, city of our love and our devotion. Thus, and thus only, shall each year be one of real achievement."

With high hopes, faith in its future, respect for traditions of the past, every effort must be extended toward achieving greater advantages for the citizenry of Malden. In the words of the city's twenty-first Mayor, delivered at the 275th Anniversary Celebration:

"Our city is bound to grow—its location, its many advantages guarantee that; but of more consequence is it that we ever hold true to the traditions, the high ideals, of those who have gone before so that the Malden of today may be transmitted to the Malden of tomorrow, and all the tomorrows which shall follow without a stain or a blemish."

We, who are able to claim Malden as our birthplace or have grown fond of the city by adoption, prize our heritage knowing full well that the men and women of past generations "builded better than they knew."

APPENDICES

Mayors of Malden

Elisha S. Converse	1882
John K. C. Sleeper	1883
Lorin L. Fuller	1884-1885
Marcellus Coggan	1886-1887
Joseph F. Wiggin	1888-1891
James Pierce	1892
Henry Winn	1893
Everett J. Stevens	1894-1895
Clarence O. Walker	1896
John E. Farnham	1897-1898
Charles L. Dean	1899-1904
William A. Hastings	1905
Charles G. Warren	1906
Charles D. McCarthy	1907
George Louis Richards	1908-1909
George Howard Fall	1910-1911
George L. Farrell	1912
Charles Schumaker	1913-1914
William M. Blakely	1915
Charles M. Blodgett	1916-1919
John Varney Kimball	1920-1924
John D. Devir	1925-1929
William A. Hastings	1930-1932
John D. Devir	1933-1939
William A. Hastings	1940-1941
Vernon Newman	1942-1943
John D. McCarthy	1944-1947
Fred I. Lamson	1948-1957
Walter J. Kelliher	1958-1959
John P. Donnelly	1960-1961
Walter J. Kelliher	1962-

List of Commemorative Tablets

BELL ROCK CEMETERY — Gravestone Tablet, Green & Medford Streets
    Old Sandy Bank Burying Ground on Mystic Side — 1640
        Contains the graves of early settlers of Malden and 39 soldiers of the American Revolution
        Erected by the Trustees of Cemeteries to commemorate the 300th Anniversary — 1940
        Plaque inserted in boulder . . Green & Medford Streets
        Here are buried Men of Malden who served during the Revolutionary War; 1775-1783
        Forty names with individual dates are inscribed
        Placed by Mystic Side Chapter, Daughters of the American Revolution — 1930

BELL ROCK PARK — Main Street
    Site of First & Second Meeting House
        In recognition of Rev. Michael Wigglesworth who preached here, 1657-1705
        "The Flag Defenders" Monument memorializing soldiers & sailors of the Civil War; dedicated — 1910
        Two bronze tablets: one listing soldiers & sailors who served in Revolutionary War
            Erected by: Malden Chapter, Sons of American Revolution, Deliverance Monroe Chapter, Daughters of Revolution, Malden Historical Society, & Park Commission
            The other, commemorating the Founders & Ministry; recognition of the hillside, called Bell Rock Pasture becoming public domain in 1904
        Both tablets dedicated in 1910
    Six-sided granite shaft holding plaques commemorating: Post 40 G.A.R.; Spanish War Veterans; Disabled American Veterans of World War I; Veterans of Foreign Wars; Jewish War Veterans; American Legion (monument-topping shaft-has been removed)

BELL ROCK PARK — corner Wigglesworth & Main Streets
    Arch erected to memorialize those who served with honor God and Country, World War II

BELL ROCK PARK — southwest on Wigglesworth Street
  Plaque in cement block with flag pole
  In memory of John Victor Robinson, 1869-1937, Park Commissioner & City Councilman
  Erected by Malden Park Dept.; dedicated by members of Lyran Lodge No. 113 and District Lodge of Mass. No. 2 of VASA Order of America
THE PARSONAGE — 145 Main Street opposite Bell Rock Park
  Home of early ministers, 1654-1837
  Birthplace of Rev. Adoniram Judson, America's first foreign missionary
FIRST SCHOOL HOUSE, 1712 — Dowling building, Main & Pleasant Streets
  Dimensions were 20 feet by 16 feet; sometimes used as a Watch House
JOSEPH HILLS — Main & Salem Streets
  A prominent man in Church & State; came to Malden in 1638
  Compiler of Massachusetts Laws, 1648; he named this town, Malden
  His house stood near this spot; later occupied by Dr. John Sprague, 1788-1803.
LIEUTENANT RALPH SPRAGUE — 106 Washington Street
  Erected on a portion of his vast acreage; came from England in 1629
  Prominent in Malden affairs; deputy of General Court
STATUE MONUMENT — Highland Avenue & Pleasant Street
  Erected by the City of Malden to persons who on land and sea defended the nation's honor in the war with Spain, the Insurrection in the Philippines and the China Relief Expedition; 1898-1902. Dedicated — Nov. 20, 1938
OSCAR C. WALLACE MEMORIAL PARK — hillside of former Beebe estate; Highland Avenue, Pleasant & Elm Streets. Dedicated to the last surviving member of Major General Hiram G. Berry Post #40 G.A.R. Erected by Rebecca Pomeroy Tent DUVCW — July 26, 1942
AMERIGE FIELD — Highland Avenue, opposite Clifton Street
  Boulder plaque memorializing Paul E. Hallisey for his years of dedicated public service to his ward and city; erected — 1971
AMERIGE FIELD — Savin Street & Fellsway East
  Memorial in honor of Capt. C. David Berg, his two officers, & 250 men of Co. L 5th Infantry, MNG; camped at this location from July 25 to Aug. 15, 1917 while waiting to be mustered into Federal Service for World War I; erected, 1965 by Malden Rifles Association
DEVIR PARK — Malden Street & Fellsway
  Roll of Honor Memorial dedicated to the 534 men of Edgeworth who served in World War I, 1917-1919; erected, 1920 by The Edgeworth 4th of July Association
NEAGLE MEMORIAL PARK — triangle of Fellsway East & West
  Named in memory of Rt. Rev. Richard Neagle (July 19, 1854-June 18, 1943); beloved Pastor of the Immaculate Conception Church for 47 years; loyal friend, civic leader, renowned educator. Dedicated by the Commonwealth of Massachusetts and the Malden community — 1952
EMERSON SCHOOL GROUNDS — Emerald Street & Highland Avenue
  Erected by the Italian American Citizens Club of Ward Two — 1953
  In honor of the men and women who served their country during World War II

COTYMORE LEA — Mountain Avenue, opposite Post Office
 Plaque inserted in rough stone boulder, in memory of the men who served or died in World War I from Ward Four; erected by neighbors & city officials of Ward Four; dedicated, June, 1917

ARMORY GROUNDS — Mountain Avenue, east of Post Office
 West side plaque: Memorial to 4 men of Co. L & K, 182nd Infantry-MNG-who sacrificed their lives in World War II; erected in 1948
 East side plaque: Memorial to the 17 men of Co. L 5th Reg. Mass. N.G.; erected in 1920 by Malden Rifles Association

FOREST DALE CEMETERY — at triangle just inside Forest Street entrance
 Plaque on boulder: erected to the memory of: Sylvester K. Abbott, Austin N. Copp, John M. Devir, James F. Eaton, Lorin L. Fuller, John K. C. Sleeper, Roland W. Toppan who in 1884 composed the first Board of Trustees of cemeteries of Malden. Their foresight and public spirit made this Cemetery possible

HIGH SCHOOL GROUNDS — west side, Ferry Street
 Memorial erected to men of World War I
 Erected by Usona Society, Malden High School

HIGH SCHOOL GROUNDS — east side, Salem Street
 Memorial erected to men of World War II by the people of Ward Five

FERRYWAY GREEN; LOUIS NEWMAN PARK — Ferry & Cross Streets
 Semi-circular wall enclosing a marker memorializing; Moses G. Kotler, M.D. (1896-1934); loyal soldier, faithful servant. Erected by Malden Park Dept.
 Dedicated, Nov. 11, 1936 by Malden Post #74, Jewish War Veterans of United States

HUNTING FIELD — Salem & Westcott Streets
 Memorial to 14 service men of Linden who gave their lives in World War II
 Erected in 1946 by Linden Veterans of World War II

TRAFTON PARK — Laurel & Jacob Streets
 Plaque in cement block with flag pole
 Dedicated, Nov. 11, 1936 in honor of Corporal William Austin Trafton, Co. L. 101st Infantry, 26th Division, A.E.F. Born in Malden, July 24, 1897; killed in Volunteer Raid on Richecourt, May 31, 1918; awarded Croix de Guerre with Palm. Citation-Distinguished himself by his courage at the same time inspiring his men by his own example of fearlessness. Erected by the City of Malden

 Plaques from erected markers in several wards of the city have been removed.

BIBLIOGRAPHY

Three Hundred Years of the General Court of Massachusetts, 1630-1930
Bicentennial Book of Malden: 200th Anniversary; May 23, 1849; published in 1850
History of the First Church in Malden: 1649-1959; compiled by Ruth Kimball Randall; published in 1959
Malden Historical Registers: number one through three; number seven, published in 1967
Malden Past and Present: 1649-1899; published by *The Malden Mirror*
Malden, Massachusetts: 35th Anniversary: 1882-1917: City of Malden 1892-25th Anniversary-1917: Malden Evening News
Proceedings of 275th Anniversary: May 25, 1924; published by Malden Historical Society, 1925
Memorial of 250th Celebration of Incorporation of Town of Malden: May, 1899; Deloraine P. Corey, chairman; published in 1900
The American Revolution: 1760-1783: by Bruce Bliven, Jr., published in 1958
Biography of a City-Boston: by Andrew Hepburn, published in 1966
75th Anniversary-Malden Historical Society: 1886-1961
200 Years-A Bicentennial Illustrated History of United States (2 volumes): 1776-1976, published by *U.S News & World Report,* 1973
Good Things About the U.S. Today: 1971 edition, published by *U.S. News & World Report*
One Nation Under God: by Ralph J. Pollard, published in 1972
Annual Reports-City of Malden: document #42: year, 1923
Malden Press-25th Anniversary Edition, newspaper articles
Universal Standard Encyclopedia: 1955 edition
The Key to Boston: Mildred & George F. Weston, Jr., published in 1961
Tercentenary Souvenir Program: 300th Anniversary-1949
Personal Interviews with Malden City Officials and City Departments
Scrapbooks: 1914-1950: Honorable John V. Kimball
Inaugural Addresses of Mayor John V. Kimball: 1920 through 1924
Newspaper articles and magazine articles from several publications
Requested information provided by several Malden residents and the Chancellor of the Archdiocese of Boston

LIST OF ILLUSTRATIONS

The great majority of photographs, maps, old documents and other illustrative source material included in this volume are from the archives of the Malden Public Library and the author and publishers are deeply indebted to the Trustees and Staff for their cooperation in making them available. Sources other than the Library are credited in the captions.

PHOTOGRAPHS, MAPS AND OLD DOCUMENTS

High Street, Maldon, England 4	City Hall, 1899 66
Governor Winthrop's welcome to Shawmut 6	Main hall of Malden Public Library 71
Daniel Perkins' house 7	Benjamin F. Dutton, residence 75
Hill's plaque 11	Trolley cars in Everett, 1897 77
Hills' Tavern 13	Malden in 1837 (woodcut) 78
Cover, Wigglesworth's *Day of Doom*, 1662 14	The First National Bank in 1837 (woodcut) 85
Stone town pump, 1886 18	Converse Rubber Shoe Company .. 87
Women's petition 21	Pine Banks Lodge 89
Second Meeting House 22	Account of Expenses, 1774 92
The Parsonage 24	Account of Expenses, 1775-76 94
Rev. Adoniram Judson 25	Soldiers and Sailors Monument ... 100
Ezekiel Jenkins' headstone 27	Dedication of Founders' plaque ... 101
Cover, Emerson's *A Sermon*, 1738 30	Magazines for soldiers, 1917 104
	World War I Victory parade 105
Dexter house 37	Town Meeting Warrant, 1776 108
Amended Plan of Malden (map) ... 43	S.S. Malden Victory 113
Central Square, 1869 48	Converse Square, 1948 114
Old Malden Bridge toll house 49	Veterans' housing, 1948 120
Elisha S. Converse 50	Letter from the First Church, 1784 124
Boston Rubber Shoe Company, 1853 51	"The Heritage" 127
Entrance to Columbian Hall 52	Dividend notice, Malden Bridge, 1788 132
Pleasant Street, 1867 53	
Wooden High School 58	Receipt to Jacob Pratt, 1779 132
High School Cadets, 1886 59	Bill from Jonathan Sprague, 1772 132
Town Meeting Warrant, 1774 62	

New City Hall and Civic Center 137	Maplewood Apartments 144
Davenport Memorial Home 140	Housing on Mountain Avenue 145
Housing at Cross and Willow Streets 142	Malden's Bicentennial Seal 147
Berkshire Apparel Corporation plant 143	Malden Town and City Seals 148

SOURCES OF INTERLEAF ILLUSTRATION

"The Beginnings"
   Artist's conception of first Meeting House on the Bell Rock hillside. Malden was among the first six towns to own a bell which was hung on a tripod frame for over 30 years and from which Bell Rock took its name.

"Growth"
   Malden Square looking north from a point opposite Irving Street, from a photograph taken about 1860.

"The Troubled Years"
   Dedication of plaque in Bell Rock Park commemorating the founders of Malden, from a photograph taken at the ceremonies in October, 1910 and shown on page 101.

"Rebirth"
   Artist's conception symbolic of Malden's far-reaching present-day reconstruction.

List of Illustrations

INDEX

A

Acadians, 32
AcID Center, 127
Adams, John, 12, 39; Richard, 12; Samuel, 33, 38
Adelaide Breed Bayrd Foundation, 143
Advances - last decade, 138-141
Aftermath, World War 1, 101
"All American City", 121
Allin, Marcy, 63
All Souls Chapel, 48
Amendments, 19th, 103; 26th, 140
American Antiquarian Society, 36
Americanization classes, 102
Andros, Sir Edward, 16
Anniversaries, 200th, 61, 82, 83; 250th, 81, 82; 275th, 106, 147, 148; 300th, 113-115; 325th, 146, 147
Apartment housing, 86, 120, 126, 127, 136
Arbella, 3
Armistice, 100
Arnold, Benedict, 37
Arts, 80, 81
Assessment of 1767, 33
Astronauts, 138, 139
Athletic Field, 89, 102, 113
Auditorium building, 82, 96, 106
Automobiles, 52, 76, 86, 88, 89, 104, 110, 141
Auto Tourist Camp, 88
Auxiliary Police Force, 111
Avery, Mrs. Alfred, 131, 132
Azoni, Walter T., 147

B

Babe Ruth, 110
Bailey, Timothy, 83; Mrs. Timothy, 83
Bailey's Hill, 8, 19
Ballots, armed forces, 111
Band concerts, 93
Banks, 83-86; holiday, 107
Banquet plate of 250th, 82
Barrett, William, 49
Baxter, Sylvester, 91
Beacham's Point, 36
Bell, Alexander Graham, 56
Bell, 23, 54; Maplewood, 64; Chapel, 64; Fire Station, 54
Bell Rock Cemetery, 27, 38, 42, 50, 61, 63, 141
Bell Rock named, 19; "pasture", 83
Bell Rock Park, 18, 25, 29, 68, 90, 112, 144, 146
Benson's Ice Pond, 95
Ber Boruchoff, Rabbi, 90
Bicentennial, 145-147
Bi-Centennial Book, 61, 83
Bicycle craze, 80, 88, 89
Big Swamp, Battle of, 15
"bitter conflict", 29, 31
Blackouts, 60, 110
Blacksmith Shops, 51, 52
"Black Thursday", 107
Blakeman, Rev. Benjamin, 23
Blaney, Benjamin, 34-36
Blaxton, Rev. William, 3
Blue Hills, 5
Board of Health Clinics, 113
Board of Trade, 71, 72
Book of Possessions, 7
Boston, 3, 8, 12, 16, 33, 35, 37, 39, 47, 49
Boston Gazette, 39
Boston Massacre, The, 34; oration, 37
Boston Rock, 5, 8
Boston Rubber Shoe Co., 50, 56
Boston Tea Party, 34, 146; reenactment, 146

161

Boundary changes, 6, 28
Bounty, Rev. War, 35
Boutwell, Harvey L., 106
Brackenbury, Alice, 61; William, 61
Bradstreet, Simon, 16, 17
Brattle Street Church, 42
Breakheart Reservation, 123
Brick making, 12, 13
Brother Gilbert Stadium, 110
Browne, Marcia P., 133
Bunker, Benjamin, 23; George, 23
Bunker Hill, 23, 36
Buses, 109, 123
Business Enterprises, 12, 13, 49, 54, 55, 67, 78-82, 105, 106, 122

C

Cable TV, 139
Cambridge, 36, 37, 63
Cambridge Convention, 39
Camp, Walter C., 80
Cape Briton, 32; exiles, 32
Carrington, Edward, 11, 20
Caule, Thomas, Sr., 11
Cavalry Flag, 15; unit, 15
Cemeteries, 48, 61, 63, 64, 73, 75, 107, 141
Chadwick, James, 15
Chamber of Commerce, 72, 107, 122, 128
Chamberlain, Edmund, 15
Charles River, 3, 5, 44
Charles Street project, 121
Charlestown, 3-9, 12, 13, 19, 23, 26, 36, 47, 64; road, 29; "set-off", 4, 28
Charter, colony, 3, 7, 15, 16; city, 75, 76, 104 town, 75, 119; Wm. & Mary, 16, 17
Cheever, Joshua, 24; Rev. Thomas, 23, 24
Chelsea, 5, 19, 24, 36; fire, 90
Cheverus, Cardinal, 134
Chick, Frank, 120
Chief Nanepashemet, 5
Children's Recreation Camp, 95
Church agreement, 9; division, 29
Church Women United, 132, 133
Churches, Catholic, 31, 47, 48, 125-128, 130-134; Protestant, 12, 21, 47, 48, 54, 74, 90, 125, 127, 128-131, 133, 136, 137
Circus days, 89
City Hall, 12, 55, 67, 137
City emerges, 75, 76
Civic Center, 125, 137, 138
Civil defense, 125
Civil War, The, 67, 80, 91; tablets, 68, 91
Clark, Jonathan, 65

Clean Air Act, 139
Coal shortage, 109
Cochrane block, 86
Code Dept., 119
Colony, The, before 1649, 5
Columbian Tavern, 12, 85
Community Nursing Association, 105
Company L, MNG, 95, 99
Concord, 10; Bridge, 36
Connick, Charles, J., 128
Constitution, U.S., 13; Mass., 39
Contagious Hospital, 74, 75, 100, 144
Controlled survey, 109
Converse, Mr. & Mrs. Costello C., 74, 75
Converse, Hon. Elisha S., 29, 50, 56, 69, 70, 72, 75, 76, 83, 88, 96; Mary D., 69, 88
Converse, Frank E., 69; Harry E., 74, 88; Ida M., 106
Converse, Marquis M., 87
Converse building, The, 69
Converse Rubber Shoe Co., 87
Converse Square, 18
Coolidge, Gov. Calvin, 96
Corey, Deloraine P., 82, 91, 141
Cotymore, Thomas, 8; grist mill, 8
Cotymore, Lea, 52, 95; ceremony, 95
Cox, Alfred E., 106, 107; Channing, 106; Lemuel, 42; Samuel, 49, 78
Cradock's Bridge, 8; Park, 103, 123
Crises, 1949, 112; fuel, 112; polio, 113; energy, 140, 141
Croquet craze, 80
Crown Point, 33

D

Dallin, Cyrus, 91
Daniels, Charles A., 57, 133
Daughters of American Rev., 90
Davenport, Albert H., 143; Alice M., 143
Davenport Foundation, 70, 143
Daylight Saving, 96, 141
Day Nursery, 105, 106
Declaration of Independence, 34, 39
Defense workers, 110, 111
Delaney, Joseph L., 99
Deliberative Assembly, The, 69, 72, 96, 103
Demolition of 1973, 74, 137
Denominational separation, 47
Depressions, 81, 107, 112, 119
Development of 1920's, 96
Devir, Mayor John D., 59

Dexter, John, 36; house, 37
Discipline, 31
District Court, 86, 142
District School system, 28
Document of 1648, 10
Dorchester Heights, 37
Dowling building, 28, 48, 54, 83, 104
Drinker, Philip, 8
Drop-in Centers, 127, 136
Drugs, 56, 135, 136, 140
Dye Works, 49, 95

E

Early settlers, 9-11, 13
Earthquake of 1727, 31
Edgeworth, 28; School, 31; Chapel, 131, 142
Eisenhower, Pres. Dwight D., 141
Elderly programs, 121, 122, 127, 128
Electric cars, 53, 64, 77
Electricity, 77, 78, 99, 109
Emergency Highway Act, 141
Emerson, Rev. Joseph, 25, 31; diary, 32; Madame Mary, 25
Endicott, Gov. John, 3, 5
Everett, 6, 29, 51, 69, 127

F

Fall, George Howard, 106
Faneuil Hall, 33
"Fathers of Malden", 10
Faulkner, Mr. & Mrs. John B., 131
Federal assistance, 59, 107, 109, 119, 135
Fellsmere Pond, 67
Ferryway Green, 72
Fire Dept., 53-55, 66, 125; stations, 54, 55, 89, 125
First Schoolhouse, 27, 28
First Street Railway, 52
Flanders, M. W. Dana J., 91
Forest Dale Cemetery, 61, 64, 73, 75, 107
Forrest, Gordon, 67
Fosdick, Elizabeth, 17
Foster, James, 63
Founding of Malden, 9; Founders, 10, 11, 42, 91
French & Indian Conflict, 32
Frothingham, siege of Boston, 36
Fuel crisis, 112
Fuller, Alvin Tufts, 88, 89, 106, 128, 141, 142; Peter, 89

G

Gardner, John, 69
Garrett, Edmund H., 15
Gates built, 12
Gay Auditorium, 134
General Court, 3-7, 9-16, 19, 20, 26, 29, 65, 68, 122
Gilbert, Brother, 110
Girl Scouts, 111
Girls' Club Association of Malden, 142
Global communications, 57
Godden, William, bequest, 26
Good Templar's Hall, 130
Gould's Herb Factory, 51
Government Center, 125, 137, 147
Granada Highlands, Linden, 136
Granada Theatre, 102, 105
Green, Dr. Ezra, 38; James D., 61
Greenland, John, 11
Green's Hall, 48

H

Half Moon Tavern, 12
Hale, Rev. Edward Everett, 67
Hall, Mrs. Walton S., 70
Harriet E. Sawyer Home, 103
Harvard College, 9
Haven, Gilbert, Jr., 61
Henry, Patrick, 146
Heritage, The, 126
High School, 57, 58, 65, 66, 72, 111, 121, 134, 135; buildings, 57, 59, 60, 66; band, 58
Highways, 7
Hill, Abraham, 12; Lillie A.B., 70; Moses, 65; heirs, 66
Hills, Joseph, 10, 19, 20, 34
Hill's Tavern, 12, 39, 65
Holmes, Chester W., 113; Oliver Wendell, 81
Holy Cross Cemetery, 48, 61, 64, 86
Home for Aged Persons, The, 142
Horse-cars, 52, 53, 64, 76
Horse sheds, 23
"Hospital Sundays", 72, 73
House of Deputies, 10
Housing, 119, 123; apartments, 120, 126, 127
Hurricanes, 109, 115
Hyde, Fletcher S., 106

Index   163

I

Independence, 38, 39
Indian villages, 5; deed, 6
Industries, 49-52, 79, 87, 122
Instructions, Rev. War, 38, 122
Inventions, 49, 56
Ipsen, Ludvig S., 82
Irish immigration, 47
Italian immigration, 90

J

Jefferson, Thomas, 146
Jehovah Witnesses, 130
Jenkins Auditorium, 134
Jenkins, Ezekiel, 26, 27; Nathaniel, 27
Jewish Cemetery, 63; influx, 90
Jet travel, 122
Jitneys, 65
John M. Devir Park, 123
Jones, John Paul, 38
Joslins, 79
Judson, Rev. Adoniram, 26
Judson House, 26
Junior High Schools, 104
Junior Hospital Aid, 74

K

Kelliher, Mayor Walter J., 119
Kettell's Tavern, 12, 35
Kimball, Dorothy D., 95
Kimball, Mayor John V., 95
King George III; 16, 33; James II; 17; Charles I, 15
King Philip's War, 15
Knights, Simon, 28
Korean Conflict, 115

L

Ladies' Aid Association, The, 73, 74
Lake George, 33
Lamplighter, 103
Lamson, Mayor Fred I., 114
Lamson, Joseph, 63; family, 63
Lane, Father Bernard, 127; Job, 22, 63; Anna, 63
League of Women Voters, 103
Legal tender, 9; separation, 47
Lewis Bridge, 31
Lewis, John, 61; Margaret, 61
Lexington, 35; Road, 35
Longfellow's "Evangeline", 32
Liberty Hill, 35; Pole, 35; Tree, 35
Lighting, 7, 51, 78, 99, 103, 106
Linden, 133
Logan Airport, 122
Lots claimed, 6, 8, 11
Lowell, 77; Parish, 47
Lynde, Joseph, 61; Thomas, 11, 64
Lynn, 5, 15, 64

M

MacArthur, Edward L., 106
Main St., 7, 19, 28, 31, 52
Malden Beacon, 39; Bridge, 8, 42, 44
Malden Action Home Care, Inc., 127, 128
Malden Council for Ageing, 121
Malden Evening News, 79, 105, 146
Malden Hospital, The, 67, 72, 73, 100
Malden Housing Authority, 123
Malden Historical Society, 70, 91, 106
Malden Ladies Soldiers' Aid Society, 67, 68
Malden Lyceum, 67; name, 19
Malden's attitude toward Andros, 16
Malden Product Exposition, 90
Malden Minute Men, 34, 35
Malden Musical Club, 103
Malden North End, 7
Malden Public Library, The, 39, 67, 69, 70, 111, 123
Malden Redevelopment Authority, 119, 136
Malden River, 8, 28, 44, 51
Malden YMCA, 48, 70, 71; YWCA, 133, 142, 143
Malden's military band, 10, 11; Militia, 34
Malden's reaction to Tea Tax, 34
Malden's Unemployment Commission, 107
Maldon, England, 10
Maplewood, 12, 64, 65, 77
Maplewood Hospital, 143
Marshall, Chief Justice John, 38
Mass. Bay Colony, 3, 4, 15; tribe, 5; seal, 15
Mass. Historical Society, 42
Maternity Hospital, The, 73, 74
Mather, Increase, 17
Matthews, Rev. Marmaduke, 20, 25
Mayor's Coal Fund, 109
MBTA Rapid Transit, 138
McBride, Mrs. Daniel, F., 112
McFadden Manor, 121
McHugh, Frank, 138

M.D.C. - Metropolitan District Commission, 68, 95; swimming pool, 95
Medford, 5, 19, 28, 36, 51, 68, 76, 127; Road, 8, 29, 35-37, 51
Medical developments, 140
Meeting House Hill, 18, 21, 25, 29
Melrose, 6, 7, 28, 50, 51, 65, 68, 76, 138; Cemetery, 61; Highlands, 28; separation, 65
Men of Mystic Side, 1648, 10, 11
Menotomy, (Arlington), 35
Metcalf, Miss Ena L., 70
Middlesex Falls, 5; Fells, 13, 68
Minister's "rate", 24
Military Force, 4
Ministry House, 25
Mishawum, (Charlestown) 5, 6
Monsignor Donovan Hall, 133
Moody, Mary, (Madam Emerson), 25; Rev. Samuel, (York, Maine), 25
Mount Vernon Masonic Lodge, 67
Mountain Ave., 8, 10, 52, 54, 133
Municipal systems, 51, 68, 76, 77, 87, 104, 107, 109
Mystic Side, 4-6, 8, 9, 13, 19, 28, 123; River, 3-5, 8-10, 28, 36, 42, 83

N

Nail Mill, 49
Naismith, James, 80
Narragansett attack, 15
Naumkeag, (Salem), 3
Naval forces, Rev. War, 38
Neagle, Rev. Richard, 106
Negroes in Malden, 28
New England, 7, 63, 109
Newhall, Thomas, 28
Newspaper publications, 79, 105
Niedner, Charles, 79, 112; William, 79, 96
Nixon, Pres. Richard M., 140, 141, 145
Non-Puritans in Malden, 13
North Malden, 7, 13, 49, 65
Northeast Vocational School, 123
Nursing Homes, 143

O

Oakes, Capt. Jonathan, 38
O'Brien, James family, 64
Odiorne Brothers, 49, 95
"Old Planters", 3
Old and New, 96; Motor Corps, 111
Old Ship Church, Hingham, 22
Old South Meeting House, 37

Old State House, 16
Olmstead, Frederick Law, 91
Opera House, 80, 131
Oration, Rev. Thacher, Watertown, 37
Organizations, 68, 69, 102, 103, 144, 145

P

Panic of 1893, 81
Paper money, 9
Paris Peace Treaty, 39
Park Commission, 91, 103
Parks, playgrounds, 103, 123
Parsonage, 25, 26
Paul, Eliot, "best seller", 77
Pawtuckets, 5
Pepperell, William, 32
Penny Ferry, 8, 36, 42
Perry, Eugene A., 81
Petition of 1633, 5; 1649, 9; 1651, 20; 1800's, 17, 18
Phillips, Wendell, 67
Pickering, Mary Alice, 64
Pierce, James, 65
Pine Banks Park, 82, 88, 107, 138
Planting of Colony, 3
Pleasant Street development, 136, 137
Police Dept., 55, 56, 67, 104, 125
Political liberty, loss of, 16
"Pond feilde", 7, 28
Population, 22, 28, 33, 53, 60, 67, 76, 90, 104, 119, 121-123, 145
Porter, Dr. Jonathan, 12
Post Office, 52, 85, 105
Powder Hill Chelsea, 36
Powder House, Malden, 35
POWS, 136
Pratt, Bella L., 91; Charles, 61; John, 64; Nathaniel, 83
Pratt Tavern, 12
Pre-school program, 135
Progressive Era, 86
Project Genesis, 127, 128
Prospect Hill, (Wayte's Mount), 5
Provincial government, 36, 38
Public School system, 26, 27
Punishment, 12
Puritan Colony, 3; Commonwealth, 3
Puritans, 3, 8, 16, 17, 42

R

Radio, 96
Railroads, B & M, 50, 65, 76, 77, 86, 130, 138; "Rapid Transit", 138; Saugus Branch, 76, 77, 86

Index 165

Rationing, 60, 111
Reading, 10, 15, 28; Road, 29
Recovery programs, 107, 119
Red Cross, 110
"Red School", 133
Renewal development, 119-121, 136, 137
Reservoir, Quabbin, 69; Wachusett, 87
Resistance to George III, 33, 34
Revere, 19
Revolutionary War, 17, 19, 33-35, 39, 95, 146
Richards, Mrs. Helen Robinson, 70
Richardson, Henry Hobson, 70
"Rising Eagle, The", 12, 65
Roads, 7, 12
Robinson, Roswell R., 50, 70; Frederick A., 50
Roosevelt, Pres. Franklin D., 111; rationing, 111
Rotary Club, 102
Rothe, Miss Dorathy L., 70
Rumney Marsh, 15, 19; burying ground, 24
Rural travel routes, 7, 8
Ryan, Father John, 48

S

Sabbath restrictions, 24
Sagamore John, 5
St. Mary's Cemetery, 63
St. Mary's, Charlestown, 47
Salem Plantation, 3; Road, 29, 64
Salem Street Cemetery, 61, 63, 64
Salem Towers, 126
Salvation Army, The, 96, 133
Sandy Bank Burying Ground, 8, 19, 23, 25, 51, 61, 63, 82
Sargeant building, 85
Sargeant, William, 9, 10
Sargeant, Gov. Francis, 141; John, Sr., 28
Sargent's Block, 52, 86; Hill, 29
Saugus, 5, 123
Scadan, (Maplewood), 64
Schick Test, 58
Schofield, Judge Emma, 142
School activities, 93; Committee, 28, 68, 93
Schooling before 1800, 26; after 1800, 57, 58
Schoolmasters, 26, 27; requirements, 26
School of Nursing, 72, 73
School programs, 60, 102

Schools, Commercial, 102; First, 28; Hebrew, 102; Parochial, 60, 64, 102, 120, 133, 134; Public, 31, 54, 57-60, 64-66, 86, 87, 93, 102, 120, 121, 126, 133, 135; Vocational, 123
Sections of Malden communities, 65, 121, 137
Senior Citizens' Centers, 120, 126, 127, 136
Sentry Hill, Boston, 39
Seymour, Rev. Isaac Lothian, 106
Shahan, Father Thomas, 130
Shattuck, Mrs. Harriette Robinson, 68
Shawmut, (Boston), 3
Sheedy, Thomas E., 103
Sheldon, Walter P., 17
Schubert Club, 103
Slavery in Malden, 28
Sleeper, Mayor John K.C., 67
Smallpox epidemic, 6, 86
Smith, Capt. Isaac, 38
Soldiers & Sailors Monument, 90, 91
Sons of American Revolution, 90
South Church, 29
South Malden, 29
Space Age, 138, 139
Spanish-American War, 81
Spanish Influenza, 100
Sports developed, 80
Spot Pond Brook, 8, 49, 76, 95; Water Co., 68, 69, 87
"Spots Pond", 5
Sprague, Dr. John, 38; Wm. & Dorothy, 29
Sprague brothers, Ralph, 5, 7, 10, 142; Richard, 5, 7, 10; William, 5, 10
Sprague, Phineas, 65
Springall, Dr. Thomas J., 89
Square & Compass Club, 131
Squaw Sachem, 6
Statues, 81
Stevens, Dr. Andrew J., 73; John of Boston, 65
Stock Market crash, 1929; 107
Stocks & Whipping Post, 12
Stone Cutter of Boston, The, 63
Stoneham, 28
Street Railway, 52
Suffolk-Faulkner Redevelopment, 120, 121
Sturgis, Clipstone, 91
Sumner, Charles, 67
Surrender of Japan, 112
Symphony Orchestra, 103
Synagogues, 90, 120, 125, 126, 128

Malden

T

Taft, Pres. William Howard, visit, 90
Tarantines, 5
Taverns, 12, 25, 35, 85
Taxation, 24, 25, 35, 85
Telephone, 55, 56; Co., 56, 100
Television, 115, 145
Thacher, Rev. Peter, pastor, 34, 46; oration, 37; Rev. War, 34-39; resignation, 42; Boston, 42
Theatres, 52, 65, 102, 105, 106, 137
The Masons, 91
Theology discipline, General Court, 20
Three County Troop, The, 15
Three Mile Brook, 8
"throat distemper", 31
Ticonderoga, 33, 38
Title 1 program, 135
Tolls, 9
Town Hall, 55, 57, 65-69, 75, 76, 83; occupants, 55, 57, 65-67
Town Pound, 12, 31; pump, 17
Trafton, William Austin, 99
Transportation, 7, 23, 31, 32, 51-53, 64, 65, 76, 77, 88, 89, 99, 106, 110, 123
Trolleys, 76, 77, 109
Tufts, Otis, 51; Peter, 8; Peter, Jr. Map, 28
Turner's Falls Expedition, 15
Twenty-first Mayor, 147, 148

U

Underground railroad, 26
Upham, Lieut. Phineas, 15
U.S. Frigate Constitution, 13, 49
Urban renewal, 119, 120-122, 136-138
Unemployment Commission, 107

V

V-E Day & V-J Day, 112
Victory Ship, 111, 112
Vietnam War, 135, 136, 138
"Village, The", 65; Cemetery, 61
Volpe, Hon. John A., 141
Volunteers, 110, 111

W

Waite Block, 66
Waite, Deacon Thomas, 66; farm, 64
Waite's Mount, (Wayte's), 5, 8, 10, 36, 39, 95
Wakefield, 123
War Bonds, 99, 110, 111
War Commission, 93
War of 1812, The, 48
War's aftermath, 112, 119
Washington, Gen. George, 36, 37, 39
Water supply, 68, 76
Waters, Capt. Daniel, 38
Watertown, 35, 37
Wayte, John, 10, 20, 26, 34
Webster, Joshua, 64
Weekly sermon, The, 24
Welfare & Relief Dept., 107
Wellington, 28
Wellman, Hon. Arthur H., 106; Rev. Joshua W., 131
Weltman Conservatory of Music, 103
West Kingston, R.I., 15
Wheel carriages, 23, 31, 32
Wigglesworth, Rev. Michael, 17, 23, 24; "Day of Doom", 23
Willcox, William G., 142
Winnisimmet, 5, 19
Winthrop, Gov. John, 3, 5, 68
Witchcraft, 17
Woburn, 10
Woman's Auxiliary of Y.M.C.A., 70, 71
Women's Christian Temperance Union, 69, 103, 128
Women, first in city government, 103
Women's Liberation, 68, 139, 140; Advancement, 68, 103; Protest, 17, 18
Women's 1651 Petition, 20, 21
Wooden Schoolhouses, 54, 57-59, 87
Worcester, Henry, 91
World War I; 58, 93, 95, 99, 100, 103, 112
World War II; 60, 95, 103, 110, 111, 112, 119, 126, 128, 135, 140
World War contributions, 60; tablets, 68, 91, 95, 112
Wright brothers, 139
Wyoming Cemetery, 61

Y

Years yet to come, 147, 148
Yorktown, 39
Young Men's Christian Association, 48, 70, 71
Young Men's Deliberative Assembly, 69

SEP 22 1976

STONEHAM

N84°30'E 275 poles   N28

Eel Pond

Capt Cox
Mr Lansden
Stoneham
Phineas Sprague
Wm Upham

N12E 890 poles

Bay Road
Reading Road

Nunins

CHELSEA

Long Pond

Swains Pond

N25W 693 Poles

Waits Tavern
Salem Road

N12E 740 poles

Capt Dexters

Medford Road

Tufts Mills

MEDFORD

Charlestown Road

Capt Bradburys
About 120 acres

MALDEN RIVER

Medford River

Hatches House

N32E 690 poles

Capt Blanews

Chelsea Road

N53°E 120 poles 3.5W

CHE

PLAN
Contain
including
Survey
Peter

Eel Pond A.T.P° 30.1.27
Long Pond 5.1.32
Swains Pond 6.0.24